Cultural and Visual Flux at Early Historical Bagh in Central India

Archana Verma

BAR International Series 1707
2007

Published in 2019 by
BAR Publishing, Oxford

BAR International Series 1707

Cultural and Visual Flux at Early Historical Bagh in Central India

ISBN 9781407301518 paperback
ISBN 9781407331881 e-book

DOI https://doi.org/10.30861/9781407301518

A catalogue record for this book is available from the British Library

This book is available at www.barpublishing.com

BAR Publishing is the trading name of British Archaeological Reports (Oxford) Ltd. British Archaeological Reports was first incorporated in 1974 to publish the BAR Series, International and British. In 1992 Hadrian Books Ltd became part of the BAR group. This volume was originally published by Archaeopress in conjunction with British Archaeological Reports (Oxford) Ltd / Hadrian Books Ltd, the Series principal publisher, in 2007. This present volume is published by BAR Publishing, 2019.

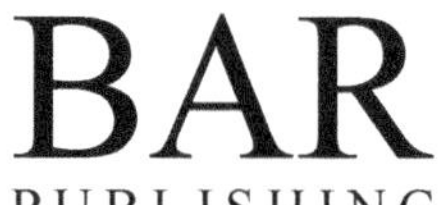

BAR titles are available from:

BAR Publishing
122 Banbury Rd, Oxford, OX2 7BP, UK
EMAIL info@barpublishing.com
PHONE +44 (0)1865 310431
FAX +44 (0)1865 316916
www.barpublishing.com

ACKNOWLEDGEMENTS

To Prof. R. Champakalakshmi for supervising this work and giving suggestions and help during the preparation of the publication copy.

To Prof. B. D. Chattopadhyaya for introducing me to the method of historical geography, epigraphy and to the epigraphical records from Bagh.

To the faculty of the Centre for Historical Studies, Jawaharlal Nehru University, New Delhi for giving me an academic insight and support during my tenure there as a student.

To the staff and Dr. Dayalan, the then Superintending Archaeologist of the Archaeological Survey of India, Bhopal Circle for sending me some of the valuable illustrations used in this work. To the Director, Archaeological Survey of India, for allowing me to survey and photograph the archaeological materials at the Bagh monastery during my field work. To the Map Survey of India, Dehra Dun for supplying me with some of the important maps.

To my innumerable friends at JNU who made my stay enjoyable and who helped with the preparation of this work in many ways.

To my parents and family and especially my late father who patiently waited to see the outcome of this work and had faith in me.

To the publishers at Archaeopress for making the publication of this work possible in an efficient and friendly manner.

While the credit belongs to others, the errors herein are mine alone.

Archana Verma
New Delhi
January 2007

CONTENTS

THE *STŪPA* AND THE IMAGE
– A SYMBOLIC INTERCHANGE IN RITUAL AND VISUAL DEPICTION

The perception of the Buddha image has gone through a number of ideational changes. The image of the Buddha itself has conveyed different meanings to the viewers in different stages of its evolution. The *stūpa* has long been thought to be associated with the *Hīnayāna* form of Buddhism, which perceived the Buddha as a preceptor, while the Buddha image has been associated with the *Mahāyāna*, which conceptualised the Buddha as a divinity. However, this categorisation of the *stūpa* and the image seems to be limited in the understanding of the symbolic meanings of these two cult objects, when we survey the archaeological data related to this subject from the Indian sub–continent. In fact, the archaeological evidence suggests that the *stūpa* and the image had a very fluid boundary of symbolic meaning and often, they were in an interchanging symbolic association. Because of this interchangeability in the symbolism of the *stūpa* and the image, it has been argued that the cult of the *stūpa* was more conducive to the *Mahāyāna* than to the *Hīnayāna*.[1] The archaeological data, which we have at hand here, reveals that often the *stūpa* served to signify the presence of the divinity – hence, its function was similar to that of an image. On the other hand, the image of Buddha did not always signify his divine aspect, but rather, it often symbolised the presence of the enlightened preceptor. In this sense, its function is similar to that of the *stūpa* in a *Hīnayāna* setting. There is another issue which is of importance in this context. The cult of the *stūpa* worship was modelled on the popular funerary cult, which revolved around the worship of the deceased ancestor or hero. The iconic tradition of Buddhism built around this popular cult as this faith extended its ritual space to include more and more of the masses. In course of time, various communities separated from each other in time and space, which followed this faith, modified it to suit their distinct personal and emotional needs. In following passages, we survey the archaeological data related to this issue in order to understand various levels of meanings associated with the *stūpa* and the Buddha image from the early historical period to about 8th – 9th c AD. This will help us to understand the artistic context in which the Buddhist iconography of Central India and Northern Deccan viz., of Bagh, Ajanta and Aurangabad developed.

(I)

The closing centuries before the Christian Era seem to have been ambivalent towards the representation of the Buddha image. This was the time which just preceded the stage when the icon of Buddha as a divinity began to be made on a large scale. *Stūpa* was still the object of worship in the last centuries before the Christian Era. For example, at Chilas II, a large mass of highly polished rock formations on the left bank of Indus, just below the city of Gandhara, were found a large number of petroglyphs of symbols, especially of *stūpa* forms by Martha L. Carter.[2] This site lacks the anthropomorphic depiction of Buddha images. However, datable to the first half of the 1st c AD, i.e., not far removed from the Chilas II depictions, we have the reliquary from Bimaran,[3] which shows Buddha wearing a *sanghāṭi* with his hand in *Abhaya Mudrā* and Indra and Buddha turned towards him. In fact, this reliquary represents the iconographic theme of the earliest Buddhist images from the Gandharan region (mostly from Swat), which show a meditating Buddha under the *Bodhi* tree, with Brahma, Indra and other divinities

[1]For example, see J Ebert, "*Parinirvāṇa* and the *Stūpa*" in AL Dallapiccola et al (Eds.), *The Stūpa, Its Religious, Historical and Architectural Significance*, Universitat Heidelberg, Band, 1980, p.55. For the interpretation of the *stūpa* as a symbol of the Buddha and therefore, as an alternative centre of power, see Romila Thapar, "Patronage and Community", in *Cultural Pasts – Essays in Early Indian History*, Oxford University Press, New Delhi, 2000, pp. 589 – 609.

[2]Martha L Carter, "Petroglyphs at Chilas II – Evidence for a Pre–Iconic Phase of Buddhist Art in Gandhara", *South Asian Archaeology*, Stuttgart, 1991, pp. 349 – 366.

[3] *Ibid*, Pl. 24.12; British Museum Collection, OA 1900.2-9.1.

requesting him to preach his newly discovered *Dhamma*. He is bare – chested like a Bodhisattva wearing the *sanghāṭi* with his jewellery hanging from the tree.[4]

Carter has shown that these reliefs represented a significant moment in the evolution of the Buddhist image. For, this scene provided the opportunity for depicting the anthropomorphic Bodhisattva, who had received the Enlightenment and who was in the process of making a decision about preaching his *Dhamma* to the world. Iconologically, this stage was the precursor to the later one (when the preaching Buddha with underlying associations of divinity was made). In the *Sarvastivāda Vinaya*, the Buddha gives Anāthapiṇḍaka the permission to make likenesses of Bodhisattva, but not of himself as Buddha. At Butkara in Swat, some of the earliest images are of Bodhisattvas but none of the *sanghāṭi*-clad Buddha.[5] Carter's arguments are significant in the light of the fact that the concept of the Bodhisattva is associated with the *Mahāyāna*. However, a figure of the Enlightened Buddha being requested by Indra and Brahma to preach *Dhamma* was not the focus of a direct worship, but was rather created in a narrative setting. Carter shows that up to the mid-first century, scenes of the adoration of the Buddhist symbols, particularly the *stūpa*, are known. The beginning of the Christian Era in the north western frontiers of the sub-continent still saw the *stūpa* being worshipped, rather than the Buddhist images being treated as icons.[6]

In fact, it appears that the closing centuries before the Christian era and the first century AD represented a period when the notion of the divinity of Buddha was in a nebulous form. At Piprahwa in Basti district, a *stūpa* has been discovered with a steatite vase in its core. The inscription in Aśokan-like characters refers to the Buddha as '*Bhagavate*',[7] thus implying his divine association. If the inscription is indeed allied to the Asokan script, then this evidence points to the fact that the Buddha was beginning to be perceived as a divinity even in a *stūpa*-worshipping context, well before the *Mahāyāna* took a stronghold in the society. On the other hand, we have a relic *stūpa* model made from green phyllite schist, originally interred in a *stūpa* at a site called Pannar, almost directly opposite Butkara in Swat. When assembled, the pieces comprise a *stūpa* model being worshipped by four freestanding figures at the four corners of the base platform. The Kharoshthi inscription at the base is palaeographically datable to about first century AD.[8] Of the four figures, three represent Indra, Brahmā and Maitreya Bodhisattva. The fourth figure is a later replacement and has been suggested to be the donor.[9] In the narrative sense, this *stūpa* model is allied to the early Buddhist images from the Gandharan region, where an enlightened Buddha is being requested by the divinities to preach. However, this *stūpa* model shows an iconological advance over the early Gandharan images, as here, the divinities are praying to a *stūpa* and not making a request to the anthropomorphic Buddha. Symbolically speaking, the *stūpa* here signifies the presence of Buddha and the divinities are paying obeisance to this divine presence. Two features are to be noted here. First, the Maitreya figure is frequently depicted in a Mahayanist context.[10] Second, this relic was interred inside a *stūpa*, suggesting that at the time of its internment, *stūpa* was still the focus of popular veneration, even though the relic reflects a strong Mahayanist association. The Piprahwa casket shows the divine identity of Buddha emerging even in a *stūpa* - worshipping context, while the *stūpa* model from Pannar shows a popular practice where a *stūpa* was worshipped, but the divinity of Buddha was acknowledged and hence, the *stūpa* was perceived as a symbol of this divine presence. In the earliest layers of the *Mahāyāna*, the *stūpa* was still retained as the object for veneration, as it practically served the function of an image. In the light of this practice and the evidence of the early Gandhara images of the Buddha (with Indra and Brahmā figures), it is interesting to study the *Kapardin* Buddha figures from Mathura, which are labelled as 'Bodhisattva' in the inscriptions.

[4] *Ibid*, p. 360; Pls.24.13 and 24.14. for the brief notice of the legend, see note 128 below and the related text.
[5] *Ibid*, pp.360-361; Pl. 24.16.
[6] *Ibid*, pp.362-363; Pl. 24.17.
[7] Debala Mitra, *Buddhist Monuments*, Sahitya sansad, Calcutta, 1971, p. 80. The inscription reads, "*sukiti-bhatinam sa-bhagini kanan-sa-puta-dalanam iyam salila-nidhane Budhasa bhagavate Sakiyanam.*"

[8] J. Sherrier, "An Important Relic *Stūpa* with Four Free-Standing Figures", *South Asian Archaeology*, 1981, pp. 254-256.
[9] *Ibid*, p. 255.
[10] *Ibid*, p. 255.

There has been a substantial debate about why they have been labelled as 'Bodhisattva.' But, before we discuss this, it is important to survey the evolution of this image, as has been shown by the scholars.

The debate about the origin of the Buddha image[11] was fuelled by Alfred Foucher's *L 'Art Greco-Bouddhique du Gandhara*, in which he propounded the argument that the Buddha image was developed by the Gandhara artists under Hellenistic influence, which was followed by the Mathura artists. This argument was accepted by such scholars as Benjamin Rowland.[12] Ananda Coomaraswamy was the prominent scholar who in his famous article, *The Origin of the Buddha Image* refuted this argument and forcefully argued that the Buddha image was independently created by the Mathura artists, who used the *Yakṣa* figures as their model.[13] J.E. van Lohuizen-de Leeuw attempted to show that the Mathura images were probably older than their Gandharan counterparts.[14] Majority of the scholars now accept the position that both these centres independently created the Buddha image. In 1979, J.E. van Lohuizen-de Leeuw brought the academic community to notice a group of twenty-two Buddha images from Gandhara which do not follow the Classical Gandhara style, but rather, are more allied to the *Kapardin* Buddhas from Mathura.[15] On the basis of the stylistic details, Lohuizen-de Leeuw contends that these Buddha figures were probably among the earliest sculptures from the Gandharan region.[16] He stylistically dates these sculptures in late 1st century BC and the first half of the 1st century AD. This stylistic dating is confirmed by the results of the Italian excavations at Butkara I which have yielded seventeen out of these twenty-two figures.[17] He also refers to some Mathura Buddha figures of the *Kapardin* type discovered in Gandhara.[18] On the basis of these evidences he argues that the Buddha figures were first made by the Mathura artists and then were exported to Gandhara, where they were copied by the local artists, resulting in the group of twenty- two Buddha figures. Subsequently, under the Hellenistic influence, this figure gradually evolved into the classical Gandhara Buddha.[19]

This iconographic relation between the early Gandhara Buddha and the *Kapardin* Buddha from Mathura is interesting for our discussion, when we consider that these figures are accompanied by Indra and Brahma figures as described above. Also significant is the fact that the *Kapardin* figures from Mathura are labelled as Bodhisattva and not Buddha. For example, an inscription associated with one such image says that this image of Bodhisattva was set up on the promenade of '*Bhagavato*' Buddha,[20] suggesting that there was a clear distinction in the identities of the two figures, even though the image is that of the Buddha in all iconographic respects. There has been much discussion over the reason for this label.[21] Herbert Hartel brings to our attention[22] the opinion of Ananda Coomaraswamy, who said that the term Bodhisattva in this context denoted a *Mahāpuruṣa Cakravartī* rather than the restricted identity of a Mahayanist deity.[23]

If we look at the archaeological evidence, there are a good number of findings which distinguish between the identities of Buddha and the Bodhisattva distributed over the major sites associated with the life of Buddha and datable to the first century AD. For example, at Sarnath has been found a colossal Buddha of

---

[11] For a very comprehensive overview of this debate, see JE van Lohuizen-de Leeuw, "New Evidence with regard to the origin of the Buddha Image," *South Asian Archaeology*, Berlin, 1979, pp. 377-400.

[12] Benjamin Rowland, *The Evolution of the Buddha Image*, New York, 1963.

[13] Ananda Coomaraswamy, "The Origin of the Buddha Image", *The Art Bulletin*, Vol. IX, No. 4, 1927, pp. 1-43.

[14] JE van Lohuizen-de Leeuw, *Op. Cit.*, p. 380; notes. 10 and 11.

[15] *Ibid*, pp. 381-385. A typical Gandhara Buddha has both shoulders covered, eyes half-closed, wears a non-transparent *sanghāṭi* and has a bun of wavy or curly hair, among other characteristics. On the other hand, the *Kapardin* Buddha from Mathura has wide-open eyes, wears a transparent *sanghāṭi* which covers only his left shoulder, leaving his right shoulder bare. The twenty two figures from Gandhara show these characteristics, along with the fact that their bun is often flat (*Ibid*, fig. 11) like the *Kapardin* figures and three of them show *Abhaya Mudrā*, (*Ibid*, figs. 16-17), the preferred pose for the *Kapardin* figures.

[16] *Ibid*, p. 386-388.

[17] *Ibid*, p. 386-388.

[18] *Ibid*, p. 393; figs 27-30; note 37.

[19] *Ibid*, p. 394-399.

[20] "*Bhagavato Bhudhasa cankame*," noted by Debala Mitra, *Op. Cit*, pp. 77 and 83; also see, Herbert Hartel, "The Concept of the *Kapardin* Buddha Type of Mathura", *South Asian Archaeology*, Naples, 1983, Naples, 1983, p. 677.

[21] For an overview of this discussion, see Herbert Hartel, *Op. Cit*, pp. 653-678.

[22] *Ibid*, pp. 677-678.

[23] Ananda Coomaraswamy, *Op. Cit*, pp. 287-328.

red sandstone, standing under a stone umbrella. It belongs to the Mathura school and was a donation of the monk Bala, who set it up in the promenade of Buddha in the third year of Kaṇiṣka.[24] Another such image was set up by the same monk at Sravasti on the promenade of Buddha for the teachers of *Sarvastivāda* in Kośāmba Kuṭī.[25] The name of the sect mentioned here is important, as this sect belonged to the *Hīnayāna* school. Kausambi has yielded many such images, of which three were donated by the nun Buddhamitrā.[26]

Above evidences point towards some very interesting features. We have mentioned earlier that the *Sarvastivāda Vinaya* refers to the Buddha as permitting the creation of an image of Bodhisattva but not of himself as Buddha. It is significant that the Mathura *Kapardin* figures are labelled as Bodhisattva and at least some of them were donated for the *Sarvastivāda* sect. Hence, it appears that in the 1st century BC - perhaps even earlier, when the Aśokan script was in use - and in the first half of the 1st century AD, a need was felt to represent the Buddha in his divine form. However, the cult of the *stūpa* worship and the *Sarvastivāda* tradition were still very strong. Hence, the *stūpa* was used as a symbol of the divine presence of the Buddha. At the same time, the *Kapardin* images of the Mathura school were created to represent the Buddha who had received the Enlightenment and who was on his way of preaching his *Dhamma;* and being perceived as the focus of popular worship. Therefore, it was not really wrong to label his image as Bodhisattva; i.e., 'the enlightened being'. Here, it is significant that the *Bhikṣuṇī* Buddhamitrā's donatory inscription refers to the Buddha as '*Bhagavato*', but labels the *Kapardin* figure as Bodhisattva. This shows the fluid identity of the Buddha in respect of the popular perception of his divinity in this period.

It appears that these concepts travelled to the North-West frontiers along with the *Kapardin* figures, which contributed towards the making of the early Gandharan images described above. The image of the enlightened Buddha being requested by Brahma and Indra to preach should be understood in this context.

J. C. Harle noted a figure believed to have originally belonged to Peshawar region,[27] which shows an iconological advance over the early Gandharan figures discussed above. Harle dates the Peshawar image in the Kaṇiṣka Era.[28] The image is in high relief, showing Buddha sitting on a lotus under a tree in *Dharmacakra Pravartana Mudrā.* He has a halo around his head. He is flanked by Indra and Brahmā leaning forward; and Avalokiteśvara and Maitreya Bodhisattvas.[29] Avalokiteśvara is identified by the small, seated Tathāgata in the crest of his turban and Maitreya, by the lock of hair on his forehead which makes a figure of eight.

Here, the Buddha is already preaching and has a halo around his head, thus indicating his divine status. The attitude of Indra and Brahmā in this case therefore, should be read as that of obeisance rather than of a request to preach. The iconographic features of the two Bodhisattvas show an understanding of the distinguishing features of these Mahayanist divinities. Though the composition of this panel is similar to that of the early Gandharan sculptures described above in terms of its contents, the meaning of the depiction has entirely changed, as it has placed Buddha in the form of a divine preacher in the context of the Mahayanist worship system. Harle says that there is another image from Sahri-Bahlol, now in the Peshawar Museum, which is almost identical with the image under discussion, except that the position of the two Bodhisattvas is reversed.[30] While the worship of the *stūpa* in place of an anthropomorphic icon continued, 1st century AD also saw the attempts at creating the image of the Buddha which could answer to his conceptualisation as a great being with a divine status.

It has been noted that when an image of Buddha was installed in a Buddhist centre, it was always associated with a *stūpa*. Karel R. van Kooij has shown in a survey that almost all the early Buddha images were installed in a

[24] Noted by Debala Mitra, *Op. Cit*, p. 67.
[25] *Ibid*, p. 77 .
[26] *Ibid*, p. 83.

[27] JC Harle, "A Hitherto Unknown Dated Sculpture from Gandhara-A Preliminary Report," *South Asian Archaeology*, Leiden, 1973, pp. 128-135.
[28] *Ibid*, p. 129.
[29] *Ibid*, p. 132-133.
[30] *Ibid*, p. 133; Peshawar Museum no. 1527.

stūpa environment.[31] He gives the reference of three Buddhist sites in Andhra Pradesh which reflect the context in which the early Buddha images were located. The first of these is a small site at Thotlakunda, situated on a hill about 15 kms. from Vishakhapatnam. In 1987 the Archaeological Survey of India excavated the remains of a small monastery, consisting of a main *stūpa*, some votive *stūpa* and some residential cells and congregational halls.[32] The monastery was in use in the 1st century AD, as is evident from the Roman and Sātavāhana coins discovered here. However, no Buddha images were discovered.[33]

Another site, Ramatirtham is about 70 kms. from Vishakhapatnam. Alexander Rea excavated this site between 1909 and 1911, in which a main *stūpa*, assembly halls and residential cells were found.[34] Kooij says that the archaeological remains here are datable to 2nd and 3rd c AD[35] i.e., a little later than the period we have mentioned above. Here, the halls contain a *stūpa* as the focus of worship. Inside the *stūpa* of hall no. 1, a relic casket was found.[36] Only one Buddha image was found at this site, stylistically related to Nagarjunakonda sculptures, outside the entrance of *caitya* hall no. 2.[37] Kooij notes that that since the apse of this hall still contains the remains of a *stūpa*, this Buddha image could not have been located in the centre of this apse, but was perhaps originally installed against the *stūpa*.[38]

Even in the 2nd-3rd c AD, the cultic object seems to have been the *stūpa*, though images of Buddha were beginning to be installed against the drum of the *stūpa*. Here, it is significant that one *stūpa* at Ramatirtham had a relic casket inside and the other *stūpa* had a Buddha image installed against it. Symbolically, the relic casket defines the *stūpa* as the embodiment of the presence of Buddha. The image installed against the *stūpa* accentuates this symbolism, as it is the visual depiction of the presence of the Buddha.

The third site discussed by Kooij, Salihundam is about 120 kms. from Vishakhapatnam. Its architecture is datable to 1st-4th c AD.[39] Here, the left hall originally contained a Buddha image, while another apse contains a *stūpa*.[40] This again shows an interchangeable symbolism between the *stūpa* and the image.

A related evidence in this connection comes from Kushinagar, an important Buddhist site near Kasia, 22 miles north-east of Deoria and 34 miles east of Gorakhpur. This site is associated with the *Mahāparinirvāṇa* of Buddha. There is a shrine in front of the *Nirvāṇa Caitya*, the most prominent monument here. Excavation of the *stūpa* disclosed at a depth of 34 ft. the circular plinth of a small *stūpa*, 9 ft. 3 in. high with a niche in the western façade having a terracotta figure of the Buddha in *Dhyāna Mudrā*, stylistically ascribed by Debala Mitra to 1st c AD.[41] The small *stūpa* with a Buddha figure in one niche creates a visual contiguity between the *stūpa* and the image, pointing to the fact that they both represent the presence of the Buddha. The Buddha figure in the niche indicates his deified status, though it is significant that it has been installed in a *stūpa*-worshipping environment, as the focus of worship here is the *Nirvāṇa Caitya*, inside which these votive remains are found. The votive *stūpa* in this case is especially important as it also signifies the presence of the Buddha's remains inside the *stūpa*, thus indicating the *parinirvāṇa* aspect.

As we have mentioned earlier, it has been suggested by scholars that the cult of the *stūpa* worship was initially related to the funerary tradition, the location being marked by a man-made tumulus. In Peninsular India the Buddhist sites often occur on or near megalithic burials. These sites maintained the continuity in the associations of the sacred, as the community which built the megalithic burials also donated to the Buddhist religious establishments and worshipped the *stūpa*.[42] The popularity of the cult of the *stūpa* was in this sense, especially significant as it pointed to

---

31 Karel R. van Kooij, " The Architectural context of the Early Buddha Image," *South Asian Archaeology*, Stuttgart, 1991, pp. 511-528.

32 *Ibid*, p. 513.

33 *Ibid*, p. 515.

34 *ARASI*, 1910-11, pp. 78-88.

35 Karel R. van Kooij, *Op. Cit*, pp. 516-517.

36 *Ibid*, p. 517.

37 *ARASI*, 1910-11, p. 81.

38 n. 36 above.

39 R. Subrahmanyam, *Salihundam-A Buddhist site in Andhra Pradesh*, Andhra Pradesh Archaeological Series 17, Hyderabad, 1964, pp. 7-9.

40 Karel R. van Kooij, *Op. Cit*, p. 519; *ARASI*, 1919-20, p. 30.

41 Debala Mitra, *Op. Cit*, p. 70.

42 Romila Thapar, *Op. Cit*, p. 596.

the reminiscences of a tradition which worshipped the dead ancestor or a hero. In the case of the Buddha the worship was directed towards an exalted personage who had attained the *nirvāṇa* and gradually, his identity was changed to a divinity. The ritualistic meaning in the two traditions was thus, contiguous.

Sites like Amaravati, Nagarjunakonda and Goli in Andhra Pradesh too reflect the installation of Buddha images in a *stūpa*-worshipping environment. Amaravati is situated on the southern bank of Krishna River 16 miles to the west of Guntur. Known as Dhanyakataka, it had begun to serve as the capital of the Andhra kings from the end of 1st century AD onwards. The *Mahācaitya* at this site was built during the period between 200 BC and 250 AD. The sculptures at this place have been divided into four phases.[43] In the first phase covering the 2nd century BC, low relief figures and animal motifs are found. In the second period covering about 1st c AD, scenes from the life of Buddha are depicted. However, Buddha is represented in these scenes only symbolically. For example, a throne under a Bodhi tree symbolises Enlightenment, a throne under a wheel depicts the *Dharmacakrapravartana* event and a *stūpa* symbolises the Buddha in his *nirvāṇa* state. Lotus flower arising from a vase symbolises the birth of the Buddha.[44]

Of special note in this class are the two panels from the Amaravati *Stūpa*, now in the British Museum, which depict the Buddha symbolically, i.e., as a throne in one case and as a throne under the Bodhi tree in another case. What is remarkable here is the fact that these panels focus on the worship of the Buddha who has attained Enlightenment, though he is represented symbolically. In yet another Amaravati panel in the British Museum collection (Figure F), the Buddha is represented in human form, but again the focus is on his popular worship. This implies that the transition from the symbolic depiction to the anthropomorphic depiction of the Buddha was not really a pointer to the transition in the way the Buddha was visualised; he had commanded popular worship even in the aniconic stage of the Buddhist art, his anthropomorphic depiction only strengthened his iconisation further.

In this period, we find three figures of the Buddha in human form.[45] In the 3rd period i.e., between 150 and 200 AD, the inner side of the *pradakṣiṇā* is decorated with the scenes from the Buddha's life and the *Jātakas*. In a scene depicting Nalagiri's subjugation, Buddha is symbolically represented as a pillar of fire. Although the tradition to depict the Buddha symbolically is still very strong in this period, now we find a tendency to include the act of surveying the events from the life of the Buddha as an important part of the *pradakṣiṇā* ritual. There is also a growing popularity of the cult of the Bodhisattvas, as is reflected from the depiction of the *Jātakas*, which also form a part of this *pradakṣiṇā* ritual.[46]

Regarding the symbolism of a throne depicted under a Bodhi tree, which signified Enlightenment, we have some interesting evidences from Ceylon, brought to our notice by S. Bhandarnayake.[47] Surveying the shrines known as '*Bodhigharas*' at Nillakagama and other places, Bhandarnayake has shown that these shrines were built around a Bodhi tree as the main cult object. The inscription at Nillakagama fixes the date of the shrine as 8th or 9th century AD.[48] Some of the important characteristics of these *Bodhigharas* were the tree as the central cult object, an orientation towards the four cardinal directions accompanied by four entrances into the shrine

[43] A Aiyappan and PR Srinivasan, *Story of Buddhism with Special Reference to South India* (In Commemoration of the 2500th Buddha Jayanti Celebrations at the Madras Museum, May 1956), Department of Information and Publicity, Govt. of Madras, Madras, 1960, p. 39. Other significant writings on Amaravati are C. Sivaramamurti, *Amaravati Sculptures in the Madras Government Museum*, Bulletin of the Madras Govt. Museum, New Series, Vol. IV, Madras, 1956 and Jas Burgess, *Buddhist stūpas of Amaravati and Jagayyapeta in Krishna District Madras Presidency, Surveyed in 1882*, Indological Book House, Varanasi, 1970; Robert Knox, *Amaravati: Buddhist Sculptures from the Great Stūpa*, British Museum Press, London, 1992.

[44] A. Aiyappan and P. R. Srinivasan, *Op. Cit.*, pp. 39-40.

[45] For references to the Buddha images found at Amaravati, vide *Madras Archaeological Report*, 1907-8, p2; *Annual Report of the Archaeological Survey of India*, 1905-6, Pl. Li; for bronze images found at this site, *Ibid*, 1908-9, Pl. XXVIII.

[46] For other comparable Buddhist remains in Andhra Pradesh, vide KR Subramanian, *Buddhist Remains in Andhra and the History of Andhra Between 225 and 610 AD*, Diocesan Press, Vepery, Madras, 1932.

[47] S. Bhandarnayake, "Buddhist Tree-Temples in Sri Lanka", *South Asian Archaeology*, Leiden, 1973, pp. 136-160.

[48] *Ibid*, p 141.

and four altars, often with Buddha images, placed around the central sanctum.[49] Bhandarnayake also refers to another type of shrine in connection with these tree-temples. Known as *Āsanagharas*, these shrines have a throne as the principal cult object. Bhandarnayake suggests that these *Āsanagharas* were in fact tree-temples with a single massive throne under the tree and with both the temple and the tree serving as the principal cult objects. In effect, this was an extension of the folk cult involving the tree worship, accommodated in Buddhism with Buddhist symbolic associations. Bhandarnayake cites the example of the Barhut relief, now in the Calcutta Museum, depicting the Mahābodhighara at Bodhgaya. This depiction clearly shows a throne at the foot of the tree, both serving as aniconic symbols of the Buddha. The later tower-temple at Bodhgaya was known as the *Vajrāsanagandhakuṭī* i.e., "the perfumed chamber of the *Vajra* throne."[50] The Ceylonese examples have a parallel in the Buddhist centre associated with Buddha's Enlightenment. While the worship ritual in these shrines follows the aniconic tradition of Buddha's depiction, at the same time, it also accommodates the images on the altars in the four cardinal directions. The ritual thus, reinforces the contiguity between the aniconic symbol and the image through its shrines. The iconographic depiction of the Enlightenment scene at Amaravati appears to be related to this worship tradition.

Coming back to Amaravati, in the last period, i.e., covering 200-300 c AD, again we find a predominance of the symbolic representation of the Buddha in the scenes from his life, though in the Temptation scene and as a child beneath the tree he is depicted in the human form.[51] There is the important evidence of the representation of the Amaravati *Stūpa* in the British Museum, which shows this *Stūpa* in relief, with the figure of the standing Buddha in a niche on the drum of the *Stūpa*, flanked by the worshipping figures. There are more seated Buddha figures in various *Mudrās* carved around the drum in the upper register. This carving clearly shows that the centre of worship at this site was the *Stūpa*, the Buddha images only finding a place against this centre of worship. The worship of the Buddha in the symbolic form, the worship of the *stūpa* and the worship of the image thus, form a symbolic continuum in the worship system in early Buddhism.

Nagarjunakonda in the Palnad taluk of Guntur district was known to the Buddhist tradition as Sriparvata and was associated with the *Mādhyamika* teacher Nagarjuna.[52] In March 1926, AR Saraswati discovered here some marble pillars and brick mounds datable to the 2nd and 3rd c AD.[53] AH Longhurst excavated the ruins here between 1927 and 1931. He discovered a large *stūpa*, eight smaller *stūpas*, four monasteries, apsidal halls etc. Several life size statues of Buddha and relic caskets of gold and silver, one of which was said to contain a bone relic of Buddha himself, were found; apart from engravings depicting the footprints of the Buddha.[54] A very important sculptural fragment from Nagarjunakonda reflects the ways in which the Buddha was perceived and represented. This fragment shows two horizontal panels, depicting the departure of Siddhartha and the temptation by Mara. These panels depict the Buddha in the anthropomorphic form. Besides, he is depicted as an exalted figure by showing a *Yakṣa* holding a parasol over his head in the departure scene. Other *Yakṣas* hold up the feet of his horse and his attendants to avoid waking up the guards of the palace.[55] Clearly, this sculpture shows the near divine status of Siddhartha before his Enlightenment and points towards the embellishment of an already well-known legend about the Buddha's life. However, the excavated materials show that the focus of worship at this place was the *stūpa*, even though the Buddha was beginning to claim an exalted status in the popular minds.

---

49 *Ibid*, pp 145-146.

50 *Ibid*, p 153; P. Myer, "The Great Temple at Bodh-Gaya", *The Art Bulletin*, Vol. XL, 1958, p. 278.

51 *Ibid*, p 40.

52 For other writings on the remains at Nagarjunakonda, see Amita Ray, "Sculptures of Nagarjunakonda," *Marg*, Vol. XVIII, No. 2, March, 1965, pp. 4-43; K. Krishna Murty, *Nagarjunakonda A Cultural Study*, Concept Pub. Co., Delhi, 1977; A. H. Longhurst, "The Great *Stūpa* at Nagarjunakonda in South India," *Indian Antiquary*, Vol. LXI, pp. 186-192.

53 N44 above, pp. 41-43.

54 *Ibid*, pp. 42-43.

55 The sculpture is a part of the Fletcher Fund, 1928 in the Metropolitan Museum of Art, New York; see Steven M. Kossak and Edith W. Watts, *The Art of South and South East Asia: A Resource for Educators*, The Metropolitan Museum of Art, New York, 2001, p. 71, Fig. 5.

In Palnad taluk of Guntur district, Joveau-Dubreuil excavated in 1926 the ruins of a *stūpa*. It contains the scenes of Buddha's life and the *Jātaka* stories. The sculptures, datable to about 250 AD, are allied to the fourth period of Amaravati.[56]

In all the above examples, we see a stage when the human figure of the Buddha was beginning to be depicted, but the focus of worship is always a large *stūpa*. The Buddha image or his figure in human form is always depicted against the background of this cult of the *stūpa* worship. In this sense, the image and the *stūpa* carry parallel symbolisms, with the underlying implication that the image is a visual accentuation of the *stūpa*. In places where a relic casket is found, often with the assertion that it contains the relic of the Buddha himself; the relic underlines the implication that the Buddha is himself present at the site of the *stūpa* and therefore, the *stūpa* commands worship from the devout populace. Kooij says that at Amaravati we have reliefs showing Buddha images on the four corners of the *stūpa*.[57] Just like Salihundam's example cited above, Nagarjunakonda contains the *stūpa* in one hall and the Buddha image in another.[58] The cult object in these places and also in other places in Deccan was always the *stūpa*. When the image did appear in these places, it was either combined with the *stūpa* or was placed in small chapels outside the main shrine.[59] At Butkara, the early Buddha images datable to the 1st c AD are all set against a *stūpa*-worshipping environment. These images were either set against the drum of the *stūpa* or installed in small subsidiary shrines, forming a square or a circle around the central *stūpa*. Dharmarajika *stūpa* in Taxila is a good example of this, as well as the Bimaran relic (Figure A), which shows this equation between the image and the *stūpa* in the votive form.[60] A small votive *stūpa* belonging to the Kuṣāṇa period illustrates the position of the Buddha images on the four sides of the drum.[61]

(II)

From 4th – 5th century AD onwards, we begin to notice the ways in which a predominant iconic phase of Buddhism accommodated the *stūpa* cult within its ritual space. For, this was the period when the Buddha image was perfected and created for an audience over a large geographical area. Sarnath, one of the major centres for evolving a distinct style in the creation of the Buddha image in the Gupta period, presents a very interesting spectrum of the *stūpa*-image symbolic parallel. The most prominent sacred structure at Sarnath, the Dhamekh *stūpa*, was provided with eight arched projections against the drum, each with a niche for an image. Also, in the main shrine at Sarnath, the three outer walls have small chapels, designed to contain images. The shrine itself is surrounded by a number of votive *stūpas*. The approach to the court in front of the main shrine is flanked by a number of structures, mostly *stūpas*. The cult object inside the shrine however, was not found.[62] In the time of Hiuen Tsang, when the cult of worshipping the Buddha image inside a shrine had become an established practice, we have a reference from the Chinese pilgrim that he saw a 200 ft. high temple at Sarnath which housed a life-size brass (bronze?) image of the preaching Buddha. This shrine may be the same as the one mentioned earlier in this chapter.[63]

Whether the cult object inside the shrine at Sarnath was a *stūpa* or an image, it is obvious that the predominant object, which received the popular worship at Sarnath, was the *stūpa*, the Dhamekh *Stūpa* being its most imposing example. The niches for images against the drum of the Dhamekh *Stūpa* and the clusters of the votive *stūpas* around the shrine only reinforce the symbolic congruity between the image and the *stūpa*.

However, in the Gupta period, the need for the creation of a deified image of the Buddha had become very powerful and Sarnath was one of the primary centres for fulfilling this need. The presence of a shrine with chapels for images despite the already existing Dhamekh *Stūpa* was an outcome of this, even though the cult of the *stūpa* worship was predominant here.

[56] *Ibid*, pp. 44-45.
[57] Karel R. van Kooij, *Op. Cit*, p. 521.
[58] *Ibid*, p. 519.
[59] *Ibid*, p. 521.
[60] *Ibid*, pp. 521-523.
[61] *Ibid*, p. 523.

[62] Debala Mitra, *Op. Cit*, pp. 67-68.
[63] *Ibid*, p.68.

At Sanchi, another predominant Buddhist centre with a great *stūpa*, we find the last additions to *Stūpa* I being made in the Gupta period. Four seated figures of the Buddha, each under a canopy were installed against the drum of the *stūpa*, facing the four entrances.[64] Here too, the main cult object remains the *stūpa*, though Buddha images are installed against the *stūpa*, to symbolise the parallel between the two.

We had mentioned earlier that at Kushinagar, a plinth of a votive *stūpa* with a niche and a terracotta image datable to 1st century AD was found in the core of the *Nirvāṇa Caitya*.[65] In the same *stūpa*, at a depth of about 14 ft. from the top, was found a circular brick chamber accommodating a copper vessel which contained a charcoal, cowries etc. and two copper tubes. One of these yielded ashes and a silver coin of Kumāragupta I, among other things. The coin and the inscription in Gupta characters on the sealing of the vessel suggest a Gupta period dating. The inscription says that the copper vessel was deposited in the *Nirvāṇa Caitya* by Haribala.[66] The shrine in front of the *stūpa* houses a large sandstone image of Buddha in *Parinirvāṇa Mudrā*, with three mourning figures. The inscription states that the image was gifted by the *Mahāvihārasvāmin* Haribala, who should be identified with the donor of the copper-plate mentioned above.[67]

The above-mentioned evidences are obviously related to the significance of this site, which is associated with the *Parinirvāṇa* of the Buddha. But, what is significant for our study is the fact that a vessel containing ashes was interred inside the *stūpa*. This defined the *stūpa* as the embodiment of the Buddha's remains. Besides, a shrine with the Buddha's image was erected outside the *stūpa*. The *Parinirvāṇa* image in the shrine hence, is the iconographic parallel of the relic placed inside the *stūpa*.

From the early phase of the Gupta period onwards, we begin to notice another trend which reinforces the symbolic parallel between the *stūpa* and the image. One of the prominent examples of this again comes from Sarnath. Excavations of the numerous *stūpas* near the court of the main shrine revealed Buddha images.[68] This is an advancement over the Kusana period finding at Kushinagar, where a terracotta image was installed in a niche against the drum of a votive *stūpa* in the core of the *Nirvāṇa Caitya*. The Sarnath finding underlines the presence of Buddha inside the *stūpa* in his anthropomorphic form, while at Kushinagar this symbolic presence of the Buddha was indicated only in an oblique manner. Sarnath in this sense creates a direct visual statement that the *stūpa* is the same as the image of the Buddha.

John Marshall, inside the *Stūpa* No. 14 at Sanchi, had found a Buddha image in *Dhyāna Mudrā* in the early Gupta style. He also refers to similar findings at Sarnath and Saheth-Maheth i.e., ancient Sravasti. At Sanchi again, *Stūpa* Nos. 12 and 14 revealed Buddha images datable to 7th c AD.[69] This trend travelled as far as Borobodur, where Buddha statues inside *stūpas* are found,[70] as we will see later in this chapter.

At least from 7th century onwards, the practice of installing an image inside the *stūpa* gave rise to a new element in the Buddhist worship ritual. Shoshin Kuwayama has brought to our notice two bronze *stūpa* models in private collectors' possession in Japan, but said to come from North Pakistan.[71] Each *stūpa* model is composed of two parts - a lid designed as the *stūpa* from drum upwards and a lower round base which supports the statue inside, which is a Buddha in *Bhumisparśa Mudrā*, seated on a pedestal supported by the raised bottom of the model. Kuwayama says that raising the bottom

[64] *Ibid*, p. 97.

[65] N. 41 above.

[66] Debala Mitra, *Op. Cit*, p. 70.

[67] *Ibid*, p. 70.

[68] *IAR*, 1963-64, pp. 92 and 107 Pl. LXI.

[69] John Marshall, *Monuments of Sanchi*, Probsthain, London, pp. 40 ff. For other references on Sanchi, vide John Marshall, *A Guide to Sanchi*, Manager of Publications, Delhi, 1936 (1st published 1918); Fred C. Maisey, *Sanchi and its Remains*, Degaun Paul, London, 1892; Ramaprasad Chanda, *Dates of the Votive Stūpas at Sanchi*, Memoirs of the Archaeological Survey of India, I, Superintendent Government Printing, Calcutta, 1919; Vidya Dehejia (Ed.), *Unseen Presence; The Buddha and Sanchi*, Marg Publication, Bombay, 1996.

[70] Shoshin Kuwayama, "Two Bronze Stūpa Models from Northern Pakistan", *South Asian Archaeology*, Monograph in World Archaeology No. 14, Wisconsin, 1989, p. 405.

[71] *Ibid*, pp. 403-406; Model B has Kharosthi inscription, suggesting its origin in the north-western part of the subcontinent, *Ibid*, p. 403.

was aimed at showing the entire body of the Buddha when the lid was opened.[72]

The *Bhumisparśa Mudrā* became popular in Eastern India from about 7th century AD and it was frequently represented in the Pāla region between 9th and 11th centuries AD. On the basis of this, Kuwayama dates these *stūpa* models to later Indian Buddhism. He also refers to a *stūpa* model concealing an *Akṣobhya* Buddha from Nagapattinam, datable to the 13th century AD.[73]

The above references show that in the Gupta period, the growing idea of worshipping the deified Buddha coexisted with the tradition of *stūpa* worship, the image worship gradually growing in popularity. Gradually, the votive *stūpa* models with Buddha figure inside evolved by combining the two forms of worship. The raised bottom of the model suggests a growing need to project the Buddha in the deified form. For all practical purposes, the votive model was a device to facilitate the worship ritual involving the Buddha image, the creation of a portable model facilitating the use of this practice across a wide geographical space. However, the fact that this votive icon was concealed inside a *stūpa* model shows that the image was perceived as contiguous with the *stūpa*, which symbolised the presence of the Buddha.

In this context, Kooij refers to a passage from *Saddharmapuṇḍarīka*, where it is stated that when Buddha opened the door of the 'Jewelled *Stūpa*,' a *Prabhūtaratna* Buddha was seen seated on a lion throne in the core of the *stūpa*.[74]

This reference underlines the idea that the *stūpa* is really an embodiment of the Buddha himself. The fact that it was said to be shown by the Buddha himself, adds sanctity to this belief. Also, it is important to note that this is a prominently Mahayanist reference. This textual reference serves to reinforce the ritual value of the iconographic examples found in stone and in votive form cited above.

In the context of the votive images of the Buddha combined with the *stūpa*, a very important reference is that of what is known as the Licchavi *Caityas* in early Nepalese art. These are elegantly carved stone *caityas* found in the Nepal Valley, which have niches carved against them. However, these niches are mostly found to be empty and therefore, have been subject to a lot of controversy regarding the reason for having empty niches. A very prominent cause that has been often forwarded is vandalism by the rival faiths like Islam. Ian Alsop however, rejects these causes on the basis of the fact that there is no sign of destruction in the niches and that the niches are empty even in areas where the invading forces did not have any access.[75] Alsop suggests an alternative cause for these empty niches, which is very interesting for our study. He gives the evidence of a small metallic Ratnasambhava Buddha figure in the Pritzker collection at Chicago, which sits inside a niche. Alsop says that the size and the shape of the figure make it obvious that it was once inserted in a niche. He is of the opinion that such figures were inserted into the niche only temporarily during the performance of the rituals and were later removed and kept in the security of the patron family or the monastery observing the ritual worship. If Alsop's argument is acceptable, then it throws a light on the worship environment of the *Mahāyāna* Buddhism, for Ratnasambhava is a *Dhyānī* Buddha evolved under the precept of the *Mahāyāna*.[76] What is remarkable here is the fact that while in this evolved stage of Mahayanism, the worship system had acquired a ritualistic nature and a specific form of iconography was evolved for the purpose, the location of this worship system remained the *stūpa* background. In effect, the observance of the ritual on the miniature image emphasised upon the conceptual parallel between the *stūpa* and the image.

[72] *Ibid*, p. 403.

[73] *Ibid*, p. 405.

[74] *Saddharmapuṇḍarīka*, XI; for a translation see H. Kern, *Saddharmapuṇḍarīka or the Lotus of the True Law*, Motilal Banarasidass, New Delhi, 1989.

[75] For Ian Alsop's views, see Ian Alsop, "Licchavi *Caityas* of Nepal: A Solution to the Empty Niche," http://www.asianart.com/alsop/licchavi.html; for views regarding the destruction of Buddhist figures in the niches, see Ulrich Wiesner, "Nepalese Votive *Stūpas* of the Licchavi Period: The Empty Niche," in A. L. Dallapicolla et al. (Eds.), *Op. Cit.*, pp. 166 ff.; Mary Slusser, *Nepal Mandala*, Princeton University Press, Princeton, 1982, p. 220; Luciano Petech, *Mediaeval History of Nepal*, Istituto Italiano per il Medio ed Estremo Oriente, Rome, 1984, pp. 65, 203.

[76] For the explanation of this concept, see the section on Borobodur below.

Apart from the Buddhist sites having a Great *Stūpa* against or inside which the Buddha images were installed, from Gupta period onwards we also begin to see the iconic accommodations being made in the *caityagṛhas* at the cave temples at the Buddhist monastic sites. It is worth noting that in the majority of these centres, the cult object remains the *stūpa*, while the Buddha image takes an increasingly predominant place in the cave temple.

Dhamnar in Mandasor district presents one such significant example of the accommodation of the image in a *stūpa* environment inside a *caityagṛha*. Though we find a number of Buddha images here, there is a marked leaning towards the *stūpa* as the cult object at Dhamnar. The *stūpa*-forms as well as the style of the image suggest a Gupta period dating.[77]

Of special consideration are two caves, Nos. XIII and XI.[78] In Cave XIII, in the centre of an oblong court is a large *stūpa*. At the back of this *stūpa* is an oblong sanctuary with a door and a processional path around it. In this sanctuary is a colossal image of the Buddha in *Vajraparyankāsana* seated on a lion throne, carved against the back wall. On either side of the door is a large standing Buddha. The walls of the processional path are relieved with Buddha figures in various *mudrās*, *Parinirvāṇa Mudrā* being included among them. The left wall of the court opens into two sanctuaries. One of them contains a *stūpa* in the centre. Over the doorframes too is the relief of a *stūpa*. The other sanctuary is smaller in size. It has a Buddha figure in *Bhadrāsana* carved against the back wall. The right wall has a niche which again contains a seated Buddha image.

The iconographic plan of Cave XIII described above shows a predominance of the cult of the *stūpa* worship. However, with the growing popularity of the deified Buddha image, additional sanctuaries and niches are provided with the Buddha images. The *pradakṣiṇā* around the sanctuary containing an image shows that the worship of the image and the *stūpa* was intertwined with each other. This is further highlighted by the fact that the two sanctuaries in the sidewalls contain a *stūpa* and an image respectively.

The Cave XI has a *caityagrha* in the centre of a court. Beyond this, are pillared verandahs with cells. The central cell on the left side contains a rock-cut *stūpa* with a relief of Buddha on the front. The right side also has a cell, containing two high reliefs of Buddha seated on a moulded pedestal carved against the back wall. The architrave over the pillars of the back wall contains reliefs of *stūpas*.

The cult object here seems to have been the *stūpa* and the Buddha image combined with it when the image worship grew in popularity. However, the significance of the *stūpa* never really died out, as is suggested by the *stūpa* reliefs on the back wall, even if an additional shrine with Buddha images as the cult objects was created. The significance of the *stūpa* is also highlighted by the sanctuary in Cave VI which houses the *stūpa* as the cult object.

Dhamnar clearly shows the ways in which the increasingly popular cult of the image was introduced in a predominantly *stūpa*-environment. However, it also indicates that the predominance of the *stūpa* was retained even after introducing the image worship in the monastery. In terms of evolving the specific kind of monastic iconography which created a symbolic contiguity in the image and the *stūpa*, Dhamnar sets the tone for Central India and Deccan, as we will see in the iconographic study of this region in the chapter on the iconography of Central India and Deccan.

About 22 miles south east of Dhamnar, in the Jhalawar district lies Kolvi, which is datable to the 6th century AD and later and which is allied to Dhamnar in visual depictions.[79] This place shows the growing importance of the image, though the continuing importance of the *stūpa* takes an innovative architectural form here. This place has five sanctuaries with an image of the Buddha in *Dhyāna Mudrā* carved against the wall. Two of them no longer have the original object of worship, but the image-pedestal can still be seen in them. The striking feature of these evidently image-oriented shrines is that they are shaped like the *stūpa*. Another important feature is the circular drum of the arched ceiling, which has projected

[77] Debala Mitra, *Op. Cit*, p. 104.

[78] Nos. 14 and 12 respectively of Debala Mitra, vide *Ibid*, pp. 104-105.

[79] *Ibid*, p. 136.

niches containing a *stūpa*. The third sanctuary however, is an exception in the sense that the arched niches in the drum contain images of *Dhyāni* Buddha rather than *stūpa* figures.

The prevalence of the image at this place is also attested by the fact that the last of these shrines contains a colossal image of a standing Buddha in *Varada Mudrā* in a court and further ahead is a pillared hall, the side walls to the entrance of which contain numerous Buddha figures. The sanctuary too contains a Buddha figure in the *Dhyāna Mudrā*.

The iconographic evidence from this place shows the stage when the worship of the Buddha image had taken a stronghold in the region. However, the *stūpa*-shaped shrines housing the cult image point towards the continuing importance of the *stūpa*. These shrines are symbolic replica of the *stūpa* housing the cultic image and also signify the presence of the Buddha. Thus, the devotee goes 'inside the *stūpa* to offer worship to the cultic image of the Preceptor, who resides 'within the *stūpa*.' Debala Mitra has suggested that the absence of the Bodhisattvas here points towards a Hinayanic leaning.[80] If this is true, then Kolvi is an example of the way in which the image was accommodated in an erstwhile *stūpa*-worshipping environment, though the extant images show the stage when the image worship had become popular.

(III)

If we trace the stages of transformations in the various Buddhist sects, we can understand to a great extent the iconographic evolution regarding the *stūpa* and image as described above. It was a little over a century after the first Buddhist Council that actual dissention took place in the *Sangha* in the second Buddhist Council held at Vaiśālī, in which the dissenters proclaimed that they would not regard all *Arhats* as perfect. After that, sect after sect emerged under the two broad divisions viz., *Theravāda* and *Mahāsānghika*. The former is believed to have eleven sub-sects and the latter seven.[81] According to both Pāli and Sanskrit traditions, the original school, which the Ceylonese chronicles do not count as schismatic, was the *Theravāda* or *Sthaviravāda*. It appears that the monks of the west, especially of Kausambi and Avanti founded the core of the body which differed from the dissenting *Mahāsānghikas*. Hence, it has been suggested that Theravāda had one centre in Pāṭaliputra and another centre (perhaps more powerful) around Ujjayinī. Gradually, it travelled towards South, settling around Kāñcī and ultimately gained a stronghold in Ceylon.[82] There was another sect called the *Mahīśāsaka*, whose geographical expanse was similar to that of the *Theravāda* i.e., along the Kosambi-Bharukaccha axis. It gradually extended up to the sea-borne countries. It was specifically popular in Mahiṣamaṇḍala and Avanti and ultimately it reached Ceylon. It has been suggested that the earlier *Mahīśāsakas* did not dwell upon the Buddha's attributes and probably agreed with *Theravāda* in holding the Buddha as a human being.[83]

According to the Theravadic doctrine, Buddhas possess *rūpakāya* i.e., worldly attributes and are subject to all the physical frailties of a human being. It is the attainment of the *Bodhi* that makes a being Buddha.[84]

One major sub-sect of the *Theravāda* was the *Sarvastivāda*, with its *Piṭakas* in Sanskrit. Its followers selected Mathura as its venue of activities and from there, they fanned out to Gandhara and Kashmir and ultimately to Central Asia and China. During the reign of Kaṇiṣka, it got a very strong support under the name *Vaibhāṣika*. It was the most popular Buddhist sect, with its influence over most parts of Buddhist Asia.[85]

Fa Hien noticed the existence of this sect at Pataliputra, while Hiuen Tsang found it in Kashgar, Udyana and several other places in the North-West, in Matipur, Kannauj and a place near Rājagṛha and also in Persia. I-tsing came across this sect in Lāṭa, Sindhu, South and East India, Sumatra, Java, China and Central Asia.[86] This shows that except for

[80] *Ibid*, p. 136.

[81] Nalinaksha Dutt, *Buddhist Sects in India*, Motilal Banarasidass, Delhi, 1977, p. 234. For more information on the changing phases of Buddhism, see N. N. Bhattacharya, *Buddhism in the History of Indian Ideas*, Manohar, New Delhi, 1993, pp.187-264.

[82] Nalinaksha Dutt, *Op. Cit.*, pp. 229-230.

[83] *Ibid*, pp. 130-132.

[84] *Ibid*, p. 231.

[85] *Ibid*, p. 134-136.

[86] *Ibid*, p. 144.

Avanti region, this sect was popular in most parts of India and also along the Silk Route and in the South East Archipelago.

The *Sarvastivādins* attributed to the Buddha divine, or even super divine powers. However, the *Theravādins* and the *Sarvastivādins* along with their offshoots regarded him as a human being, who was subject to all sufferings common to a pious and meritorious person. He had attained perfection (i.e., Buddhahood) at Bodhgaya[87] and was therefore exalted; and according to the *Sarvastivādins*, possessed divine powers.

The *Mahāsānghikas* did not subscribe to this view. They questioned the belief that a personage, who attained perfection and was the best of all beings in merit and knowledge, could be regarded as an ordinary human being. Hence, they contended that his appearance in the mortal world was only fictitious in order to follow the ways of the world. He had achieved all the perfections in his previous existences as a Bodhisattva.[88] This kind of conceptualisation paved the way for the evolution of the Bodhisattva pantheon in later Buddhism and also, for the deification of the Buddha. However, it should be noted that the *Mahāsānghikas* had in mind Buddha Gautama and not the countless Buddhas as conceived by the Mahayanists later.[89]

The *Mahāsānghikas* migrated from Magadha in two streams, one towards the North and the North-West and the other towards the South. The southern branches, known as the *Caityakas* or the *Śailas*, migrated from Pāṭaliputra through Orissa to Guntur district and settled there around 2nd century BC. Gradually, they extended to other hills along the Krishna River, Amaravati and Nagarjunakonda being their most prominent centres.[90]

The north-western branch divided into five sub-sects. Of these, the *Lokottaravādins* considered the Buddha as supra-mundane and propounded the concept of the Buddha as a transcendental being, thus preparing the ground for his deification which was a feature of *Mahāyāna*.[91] In *Mahāvastu*, it is said that transcendent are practices of *Bhagavān* and so are his merits and daily actions. He follows the ways of the world just as much as he follows the transcendental ways.[92] Similarly, *Kathāvastu* proclaims, "*Budhasa Bhagavato vohāro lokottaro ti*" i.e., Buddha's actions (*vohāro*) are *lokottara* or transcendental.[93] It is significant that in both the passages, Buddha is referred to as '*Bhagavān*'/'*Bhagavato*', indicating his deified status.

The evolution of the Bodhisattva pantheon was intertwined with the notion of ten *pāramitās* i.e., perfection in virtues by extreme sacrifice of one's own self. The Theravādis conceptualised the Bodhisattvas as average beings who were subject to sufferings. They had six *pāramitās* i.e., *dāna, śīla, kṣānti* (perseverance), *vīrya* (energy) and *prajñā* (perfect knowledge). In response to the ten *pāramitā* concept of the Lokottaravādins the Theravādins added four more *pāramitās* to the list.[94] The Lokottaravāda was thus, instrumental in the emergence of the *Mahāyāna* school of thought and it also influenced the *Theravāda* school.

The above sketch shows some parallels with the iconographic/cultic practices surveyed above. For example, we are informed that even before the emergence of *Mahāyāna*, from the Second Council onwards, there was a gradual evolution in the Buddhist thought which leaned towards the conceptualisation of the Buddha as an exalted being, possessed of divine powers. Hence, we have the inscription in Aśokan-like Brāhmī which describes the Buddha as '*Bhagavato.*' Also, the predominance of the *Sarvastivāda* at Mathura and its radiation from there on to Gandhara, explains the labelling the *Kapardin* Buddha figures from Mathura as 'Bodhisattva' and of the travel of the *Kapardin* figures to Afghanistan. For the Sarvastivada as we see, the Buddha who attained knowledge was not a deity but was endowed with divine

87 *Ibid*, pp. 76, 169.
88 *Ibid*, pp. 77.
89 *Ibid*, pp. 77.
90 *Ibid*, pp. 67-68.

91 *Ibid*, pp. 68-69.
92 *Ibid*, p. 107.
93 *Ibid*, p. 108, quoting *Kathāvastu*, II/10.
94 *Ibid*, p. 231-235; the four later *paramitas* are *upāya kauśalya* (devices for imparting training to the *śrāvakas* for developing their mind for the attainment of Buddhahood), *jñāna* (knowledge of the means for the attainment of the Buddhahood), *praṇidhana* (to vow to attain Buddhahood) and *bala* (to acquire enough strength to attain Buddhahood).

powers. Also important is the spread of the various sects over various parts of the sub-continent, in their various forms, some of which regarded the Buddha as a human being, some as an exalted being and some as a divine being. This led to the intermingling of these concepts which manifested in various cultic practices and their related iconographic features.

As mentioned in the passages related to Tun Huang, we have the reference of the *Sanskrit Sūtra* translated into Chinese which lays stress on the worship of the Buddha image as the only mark of a true follower of Buddhism. However, the major part of the debate seems to have focussed on the characteristics of an *Arhat*, the nature of the historical Buddha etc. and not on the cult object to be worshipped. Perhaps, this was because it was felt necessary to extend the sacred space to the popular practice of *stūpa* worship; and also, because psychologically speaking, the *stūpa* and the image signified the same thing i.e., the presence of the Buddha. In this survey, we have seen how various centres resolved the dichotomy between the two cult objects, often combining or interchanging them, the experience of China being the final culmination of this effort, where the image was predominant, but where other forms of visual symbols were used to accommodate the popular audience.

Also, the presence of an image did not always signify a deified status of the Buddha. For, even if certain sects only exalted the Buddha without deifying him, an image could still be created. However, the fact remains that the experimentations – in the realm of thought, worship ritual and iconography – were carried out only after the dissensions of the second Buddhist Council. There was after all, an aniconic phase when the Buddha was represented only by symbols and when only the *stūpa* was worshipped. This points towards the fact that with the increased need for an icon which could be perceived as exalted and which could be worshipped, the merger of the symbolisms of the *stūpa* and of the image, made it possible to converge the presence of the two cult objects in their specific forms, as we have seen in this survey.

AN INTRODUCTION TO VALKHĀ (ANCIENT BAGH) – A HISTORICAL REGION

This study concerns with the region around the early historical Buddhist monastery in Bagh, in the state of Madhya Pradesh in Central India. In the inscriptions of 4th – 5th century A.D., this area was included in the chiefdom of Valkhā, as the place is mentioned in the epigraphical records. The modern name Bagh is probably derived from Valkhā. The Buddhist monastery of Bagh lies three miles from Bagh village at 22° 22'N and 74° 48'E in Dhar district of the state of Madhya Pradesh in central India, on the left bank of Bagh river – a small stream which flows for about 35 kilometers southwards before joining Narmada. The caves are located on the southern slopes of the Vindhya hills. The cliff side, on which they are excavated, is the only outcrop of sandstone in an otherwise basaltic region (Marshall 1927: 6).

Valkhā was included in the region known as Avanti or Western Mālava in the early historical period up to circa 4th – 5th centuries A. D. various excavated sites of the Avanti region from this period show that the centres of Avanti were interlinked with each other and Valkhā or Bagh was brought into this network but not directly, as it does not lie on the major communication networks. Valkhā has not been excavated so far and hence any identification within the region of the various sites remains tentative. The present geography of the area around Bagh shows that this area lies in a sandy hill tract with hardly any trees around. However, it is difficult to say whether this area was entirely arid and sandy or covered with forests in the ancient period, as cultivated land is mentioned in the inscriptions found from the region.

Western Mālava comprised of the present districts of Ujjain, Dhar and West Nimar (where Maheshwar is located) and is largely covered by black soil, which is good for the cultivation of cotton, wheats, sugarcane, groundnuts etc. (Spate 1964: 576 – 577). Amongst the main rivers of this region is Narmada, its valley lying between the Vindhya and Satpura ranges, flat and relatively more fertile than the other areas in Western Mālava. The southern bank of Narmada is covered with forests, enclosing rural settlements amidst them, while the northern region around Bagh is a sandy, hilly tract lacking in greenery today (Map Survey of India Sheet No. 46). It is this area on both sides of Narmada over which the chiefdom of Valkhā lay. This chiefdom located in the Avanti region is little known to history except through the copperplate charters issued from Valkhā itself. However, we get many references to Avanti as an identifiable region from both the Brahmanical as well as the Buddhist sources.

Avanti had two divisions – the northern one known as Avanti with its centre at Ujjayinī (modern Ujjain) and the southern one called Avanti – Dakṣiṇāpatha with its centre at Māhiṣmatī (modern Maheshwar). It is not clear whether the tradition of Avanti – Dakṣiṇāpatha continued into the Gupta period i.e., 4th – 5th centuries A.D. (Bhandarkar 1921: 45), but since this was the southern part of Avanti, spread along the banks of Narmada, with Māhiṣmatī as its centre, one can say that the Valkhā chiefdom of the Gupta period lay roughly in the traditional Avanti-Dakṣiṇāpatha, as it had the same area of influence with its centre shifting from Valkhā (Bagh) to Māhiṣmatī in its later phase of existence.

Among the more prominent sites excavated are Ujjain, which was a walled city, its satellite sites and Maheshwar. Ujjayinī, which emerged as an important settlement from 700 B. C., had a slow pace of evolution in period I (BC 700 – 500), but showed enormous increase and differentiated pace of activity in period II (BC 500 – 200). There are marked changes in lifestyles followed in the fortified area in this period. It is also significant that this was the period of formation of the Mahājanapadas, Avanti being one of them, with Ujjaiyinī being its centre. The archaeological findings from Ujjain (*Indian Archaeological Review*, Henceforth *IAR*, 1956 – 57: 20 – 28; 1957 – 58: 34 – 36) show that Ujjayini was an important centre of power and commerce in period II. Findings of shell bangles suggest Ujjaiyinī's connection with the western seacoast of Bhṛgukaccha in Gujarat and ivory seals suggest some kind of administrative set up during BC 500 – 200. There are indications of religious cults of popular nature existing here, as the mother – goddess figurines of terracotta have been found. The cult of the mother-goddess was popular in Avanti as a whole, including Valkhā is evident from the archaeological findings from elsewhere in the region and the epigraphical records of the region, which are discussed in this work. Among the materials found in this region, most used in the second phase seem to continue into the third phase.

Dangwada, a site near Ujjain, also provides evidence of having links with Vidiśā and Ujjain and the prevalence of Yakṣa cult, a common phenomenon in the early historical period (*IAR* 1979 – 80: 54 – 55; 1982 – 83: 56 – 60). Dangwada also shows figurines of the deities of different religious faiths such as Hāritī, Buddha, Viṣṇu, Durgā, Lajjā Gaurī etc. in the Gupta period. Other sites near Ujjain have also come up similar evidences (*IAR* 1980 – 81: 39).

Excavations in the smaller sites near Ujjain show that while crafts activity slowed down in Ujjaiyinī, in some of the sites close by, it picked up pace, not only in kinds of material worked with but with a definite shift towards working in gold, silver and semi-precious stones. It may signify that there was an attempt at branching out of the crafts activity from the walled city to several sites nearby.

Although the above description does not give a full picture of Avanti as a whole, it shows the economic activity going on in the core area. The data regarding the popular, Buddhist and Brahmanical sects may be taken as a general picture of the socio-religious activity in Avanti region. Further excavations in the smaller sites may well addmore useful information to improve our understanding of the general picture.

The excavations at Maheshwar show that the material culture diminished in quantity at Maheshwar in the last phase of its occupation i.e., between AD 100 – 400 (Sharma 1990: 68 – 70). However, we know from the epigraphical records of Valkha that the base shifted from Bagh to Māhiṣmatī in the last decades of 5th century A.D. subandhu has issued two inscriptions from Māhiṣmatī during this time and his inscriptions begin with the phrase 'Māhiṣmatī nagarāt' i.e., '(issued) from the city of Māhiṣmatī' (Epigraphia *Indica*, henceforth *EI* 19: 262 – 263; *Corpus Inscriptionum Indicarum,* henceforth *CII* Vol. IV Part I: 20). The reference to Māhiṣmatī as a 'nagara' shows that the people in the last phase of the 5th century A.D. perceived this place as an urban centre. Moreover, the preference of Māhiṣmatī over Bagh shows that the former was regarded as a more appropriate place to be the centre of power.

A site near Maheshwar is Pagara where excavations have revealed several levels of occupations from 1st century A.D. to the 12th century A.D. we deal here with only the first two phases i.e., up to 6th century A.D. the first phase (i.e., 1st – 3rd centuries A.D.) shows red ware. The second phase shows a larger assemblage including shell-bangles, Gupta gold coins and Kṣatrapa silver coins (*IAR* 1980-81: 33), suggesting large-scale exchange based on trade and a link with the seacoast.

Apart from the excavated sites in Avanti, we have the names of the sites mentioned in the epigraphical sources. Some attempt has been made by the editors of the recently found copper-plate inscriptions of Bagh to identify some of these sites. However, as the editors themselves agree, these identifications are only tentative, based on the similarity in names mentioned in the inscriptions and those of the modern sites and await confirmation through excavation. The inscriptions give some idea about the whereabouts of some sites, as references to their geographical locations are mentioned. Following this method, the present work has attempted to identify a few of the sites mentioned in the inscriptions and a map has been prepared to see the expansion of the settlements in the Valkhā region over the period 4th – 5th centuries A.D.

Here, we give an idea of the method used in identifying these sites. The editors of the Bagh inscriptions have, on the basis of similarity of names, identified 'Dagdha Pallikā' as Dahi and 'Lohakāra Pallikā; as Lohari (Ramesh and Tewari 1991: XXIII). Since 'Yajñāgrāhaka' is granted along with 'Lohakārapallikā' to the same Brāhmaṇa (*Ibid*: 37, lines 2 – 6), it is probable that the former lay somewhere near Lohari. A village called 'Devāgrahāraka' is granted in 'Urīkarāṣṭra', alongwith

'Gavayapānīyaka' (*Ibid*: 15). Following this method of identification, we find a village called Deogarh, resembling in name 'Devāgrahāraka'. If this identification is accepted, then the location of 'Gavayapānīyaka' should be taken as near Deogarh, although its exact location cannot be ascertained. Again, two other sites are Gajnera (Garjanānaka) and Piplod (Pippalojjhara) (*Ibid*: 6, lines 2 – 5; 28, lines 2 – 5). Their identification is based on the similarity in names as well as on the reference of their location on the south bank of Narmada, which matches with the location of the tentatively identified sites.

Here, a special mention needs to be made of a territorial division called Navarāṣṭrakapathaka, referred to as lying south of Narmada (*Ibid*: 46, lines 2 – 6). The name suggests that this was a new territory, earlier uninhabited, which was settled by the Valkhā chiefs. Hence, the location could be either south of Gajnera etc., or either south of Talwara Deb, Ummeda, for these are areas which do not have any sites mentioned in the inscriptions.

There are still a number of sites which remain unidentified, in the absence of any clues to their whereabouts. Apart from Narmada, only one other river is mentioned i.e., Pomphagartta (a tributary of Narmada). However, no major tributary of Narmada today has a similar name. Hence, it is possible that this was the local name of one of the smaller tributaries of Narmada, now lost to us. Because of these identifications, Valkhā can be placed in the wider context of Avanti region.

This work studies the process of acculturation that transformed the profile of Valkhā i.e., the ancient region around Bagh. All the inscriptions from Bagh commence with the term 'Valkhāh' and some also give the phrase 'Valkha-Adhiṣṭhāna', suggesting that the power base of the chiefdom was called Valkha and this gave the name to the chiefdom as well (Ramesh and Tewari 1991: XXIV). This power base called Valkhā was identified with the modern township of Bagh by G. S. Gai, the editor of the *Epigraphia Indica*, Volume 37, who first published an inscription of Bhulunda, the first chief mentioned in the Valkhā grants. This is supported by the fact that the present hoard of copperplates were found buried in a field on the outskirts of Bagh and also from the fact that the Buddhist monastery of Bagh which received a grant from Subandhu, the last Valkhā ruler, is situated nearby. The similarity in names is another factor supporting this identification of Valkhā with Bagh, 35 kms. north of the place where Bagh meets Narmada, lying on the right bank of Bagh river, a small tributary of Narmada.

By plotting the tentatively identified villages mentioned in the Bagh-places on the map, Valkhā chiefdom emerges as a triangle, spreading on both banks of Narmada, stretching from each to wets between Maheshwar and the western boundary of present-day Dhar district and from north to south between Bagh and the southern boundaries of present-day Rajpur and Barwani Tehsils in (West-Nimar district. The latter extent forms the base of the triangle, which tapers towards the east, Maheshwar forming the apex (Map 2). A look at the present-day map shows that this area encompassed by the Valkhā chiefdom lay in the Narmada valley lying between the Vindhyas and Satpuras, is flat and fertile and cultivation is more extensive. On the southern side of Narmada, it is covered with forests, enclosing rural settlements amidst them spread on both sides of Narmada, the Valkhā cheifdom comprised of the present day Dhar and West Nimar district.

Historically, the region fell in Avanti, whose name has come down to us from the *Anguttara Nikāya* as one of the sixteen *Mahājanapada* (Morris and Hardy 1885-1900, Vol. 1: 213). Avanti's southern limit was the region called Avanii-Dakṣiṇāpatha, with Māhiṣmatī or Maheshawar as its chief city, since Valkhā was spread along both the banks of Narmada, with Māhiṣmatī as its capital in its 3rd phase of development, it must have coincided with the erstwhile Avanti-Dakṣiṇāpatha region of Avanti, literally, 'that portion of Avanti which led towards Dakṣiṇāpatha'. The southern offshoot of the Uttarāpatha, which started from Mathura and passed through Ujjayinī (or Ujjain), the capital of Avanti, went on to Māhiṣmatī, which was the nodal point of routes from south (Dakṣiṇāpatha), north and western sea-coast of Surāṣṭra. The term Avanti-Dakṣiṇāpatha is significant in this sense.

Ujjayinī was also linked to Vidiśā and from there on to the northern route (Uttarāpatha). These linkages show that for its economy

Valkhā could exploit the route-system through Māhiṣmatī and Ujjainī and participate in the long distance trade. The fact that the Māhiṣmatī-Bhārukaccha route passed right through the Valkhā territory is significant in this context. Perhaps, this was one reason why the centre shifted from Valkha to Mahismati in the 3rd phase, since it was easier to exploit this route and also other converging ones, from Māhiṣmatī than from Valkhā, which lay in the interior parts. Also, the ruler of Māhiṣmatī could control the granted land along the banks of Narmada. Thus one can say that the shift to Māhiṣmatī signified an increase in power for the ruler who controlled Valkhā.

As for the socio-cultural processes of Valkhā's development, these linkages explain from which centres the influences of acculturation and assimilation came to Valkhā. As will be seen, the Bagh caves experienced the advent of Mahāyānism into a pre-existing *Hīnayāna* centre of Buddhism. The long-distance connection to Bagh with Mathura, a prominent centre of Mahāyānims, via Māhiṣmatī and Ujjain, explains the incoming influence of Mahāyānism in Bagh. Thus the reference to 'repairs' in Subandhu's grant to the caves in 5th century AD, may point to this influences and an attempt at introduction of art-forms expressing Mahayanist beliefs, as will be shown in the chapter on the monastic art. Bhagh's connection with Ujjayinī, the epitome of Gupta culture and Brahmanical belief-system, also suggests that the Brahmanical acceleration of Bagh with other important urban centres is important for our study. The acceleration processes in Valkhā manifested themselves in such a form that it becomes necessary to study these processes through diverse and seemingly unrelated categories of sources and different approaches as, for example, the inscriptions from the region and the works of art found near Bagh (or Valkhā, as it was known in 4th – 5th century AD).

In order to understand the necessity for adopting this kind of approach, it would be appropriate to look at the complexity of developments that took place in Valkhā between the 4th century and the last decades of 5th century AD. Broadly speaking, the acculturation process in Valkhā chiefdom can be divided into three distinct phases. These phases, as evident from the inscriptions, show that this was one period when the chiefs of Valkhā, following the broader socio-cultural trends set by the Gupta rulers, tried to emulate them and gave a gradually increasing patronage to the Brahmanical system. This patronage had an impact on the local cultural matrix, which went out of visibility while the Brahmanical influence increased through the three phases. This influences transformed the local economic-bases, religious and social institutions.

In the first phase (AD 358-379), we see what the local socio-religious and economic matrix of Valkhā was like. We find that within this local matrix, certain features of Brahmanism had started surfacing during the first phase, although they hadn't become strong yet. It is in the second phase (AD 383-45) that this Brahmanical influence became strong – so much so that the local elements, which had occupied a major space in economy, society and religion in the earlier phase, lost patronage as well as visibility in the 2nd phase.

Here, the question arises, as to what happened to these local elements after the growing Brahmanism overshadowed them. For, certainly they must have existed even after the dominance of Brahmanism had set in, for it had been the basic element of the Valkhan society. The answer for this is found in the study of the third phase, which is shorter in duration, but important (from AD 454-487). This phase tells us that Brahmanism was not the only influence in Valkhā; it had coexisted with Buddhism – at least for some time in the second phase onwards. Only, it had not surfaced in the sources available to us form the 3rd phase, when it became important for the process of socio-economic change going on there – for this was the phase when the base of Vlkhā shifted to Māhiṣmatī, and therefore, had greater control over the Māhiṣmatī-Valkhā route which lay only 35 kms. from the centre of Buddhism in the region. The association of the traders with the Buddhist monasteries is well-known. In the third and last phase, even, the ruler wanted to relate himself to the erstwhile Valkhā centre, where the caves lie.

It is at this point that the study of the works of art of this Buddhist monastery becomes important, for not only does it provide insights into the finer details and the symbolism used in Buddhims and its art, but it also suggests that the elements of the local culture which had been over-shadowed by Brahmanical system, had formed a space in Buddhism. Thus, what appears from the combined study of the epigraphs and the monastic art from the Buddhist caves is that the local cultural elements, when they lost their support – based because of the advent of Brahmanism, turned to Buddhism, which not only assimilated some of these elements, but was also influenced by Brahmanism in its ritual and art. Thus, we find different kinds of approaches to the local culture by theses two dominant acculturating influences in the region – one competed with the local culture and tried to dominate and suppress them, while the other received them head-on and incorporated some of their strands in its institutions. Thus, we see a cultural-flux going in the region during the period studied.

The above picture shows why we need to study these diverse forms of source-materials and how they are in conjunction with each other. Without the one, we would not be able to understand the other. By studying only the epigraphs, we will not get the full-picture of what was going on here in terms of the acculturation process – it will only tell us about the Brahmanisation of the region. At the same time, by looking at only the monastic art, we will hardly understand certain peculiar traits it shows in its expression, which sets it apart from the other comparable centres, e.g., Ajanta. Thus, both these sources are needed to understand that the art-forms of the Bagh-Caves are in part a visual manifestation of the cultural-flux going on in Valkhā.

As described earlier, epigraphs form one of the major sources of information in this work. They are 36 in number, and cover a period from circa AD 358 to 487, as described earlier. A word needs to be said about the era used to calculate the date of these charters. All the Valkhā chiefs mention that they meditate at the feet of the *Paramabhaṭṭāraka,* a well-known title for the Gupta overlords, thus suggesting that these chiefs were the subordinates of the Guptas. Most scholars e.g., R. C. Majumdar and later G. S. Gai, subscribe to this view (*EI* 15: 290-91; *Ibid* 37: 243). The editors of the present hoard of copper plates too have accepted the era used by the Valkhā chief on the basis of palaeograpy and internal evidences (Ramesh and Tiwari 1991: Introduction, vii-viii), as the Gupta era. In the present work too, the era has been taken to be the Gupta.

On the basis of the above, some ideas of the chronology of the Valkhā chief may be formed. Thus, the chief of the first phase, Bhuluṇḍa ruled from the year 38 to the year 59 (i.e., circa AD 358-379), his region coinciding with that of Samurdragupta's years 16 (AD 336) to 57 (AD 377). In second phase, first two rulers, Svāmidāsa (years 63-67, i.e., AD 383-387) and Rudradāsa (years 67-70, i.e., AD 387-390) were contemporaries of Kumāragupta I (years 96 – 135, i.e., AD 416-455) (*Ibid*: viii). This shows that this group of Valkhā chiefs were subordinates of the Gupta rulers form Samudragupta to Kumāragupta I. The short tenures of the Valkhā chief also points to either a political instability in the chiefdom, (or that this being a region probably not under the traditional rule of kingship), followed by a system of rule-by-rotation of chiefs. This is suggested from the fact that Rudradāsa, after year 70 (AD 390), is mentioned again in the year 117 (AD 437) (*CII*, Vol. IV: I; 11-12) – a year which fell during the period of Bhaṭṭāraka. Thus, either a political instability or a rule by rotation is strongly indicated. If there was a political instability, then the numerous land-grants to Brāhmaṇas during this phase suggest an attempt by the rulers to create a strong support-base for themselves among the dominant social group. Thus, the cultural-flux described earlier may have been caused by a strong political factor too.

The epigraphic evidence presents the uniqueness of the third phase – the shift of the centre from Valkhā to Māhiṣmatī has been mentioned earlier. Apart from this, it is striking that the ruler of this phase, Subandhu, does not mention that he worships at the feet of the *Paramabhaṭṭāraka.* Subandhu's donation to the Buddhist caves at Bagh is similar to Budhagupta's patronage to Buddhism. The date of Subandhu's one plate is lost, while his other plate is dated in the year 167 (AD 487), thus placing him and the 3rd phase in the latter half of the 5th century AD. The date of AD 487 makes him a contemporary of Budhagupta, who ruled over eastern Mālava, Bengal, Bihar, etc. It is significant that Western Mālava, where

Māhiṣmatī and Valkhā chiefdom were located, did not fall in his region. This was the period when certain regions had started becoming independent and the power of Guptas was declining (Gupta Vol. 1 1974: 353). Thus, Subandhu might not have been a subordinate of Budhagupta, but still might have been influenced by the Gupta culture – hence, making the Gupta impact over Subandhu's domain only cultural and not political.

A detailed analysis of the inscriptions from the socio-economic and religious viewpoints prevailing in Valkhā will follow in the next chapter. Here, it's sufficed to say that these inscriptions give some data about the territorial divisions and the villages donated which may be studied here. The territorial divisions mentioned in the inscriptions are - *rāṣṭra, viṣaya, āvāsa, bhukti*, and *pathaka*. Their exact hierarchy is not certain. However, some idea can be formed going by D. C. Sircar's definitions of these terms. Here, it is important to note that Sircar gives the meaning for avasa as a shelter or accommodation which the villages were obliged to provide for the touring officers of the king (Sircar, 1966: entry under '*āvāsa*'). However, in one inscription from Bagh (Ramesh and Tiwari, 1991: *Grant of Bhuluṇḍa*, Year 55, *Srāvaṇa*, line 3), 'Durdūkavāsa' is mentioned as a territorial division within which three grant-villages were located. Here, *āvāsa* gives the connotation of a territorial division comprising of several villages – different from that given by Sircar. *Rāṣṭra, Viṣaya* and *Bhukti* are well-known as territorial divisions. The most frequently used division in the Bagh inscriptions is the *pathaka*. There are eight *pathakas* mentioned. Sircar gives its meaning as a "group of villages" (Sircar 1966: 243). Considering that this was the most frequently used term, it may be concluded that this was the division one step higher than that of the village unit. It served as the major means of identifying a settlement – it was enough to know which *pathaka* a village belonged to even if its *rastra* and *viṣaya* etc. were not known.

There is also another term used in at least one case – that of a Palli, in Dāsilakapallipathaka (*CII*, Vol. IV, Part I: 20). A *palli* is a hamlet, a village or its part (Sircar 1966: 228). Thus, 'Dāsilakapallipathaka' suggests that it was a *pathaka* which had grown from a hamlet. The sense of the expansion of a settlement is included in this name.

These references from the epigraphy suggest that Valkhā was a region showing some kind of administrative divisions, although their hierarchy is not known. Thus, an evolving polity, and an expansion of settlement is suggested by these divisions and their names. The emerging polity and its socio-religious and economic features will be discussed further in the next chapter.

In order to map out Valkhā, it is necessary to attempt to identify the sites mentioned in the grants, so that we can get an idea of the expanse of the chiefdom and also, the location of the divisions discussed above. Such a map can give us an idea of the settlement-pattern of Valkhā chiefdom. Thus, the plotting of the settlement-pattern on the map is linked to the identification of the sites. The information provided in the inscription helps us to identify at least some of the sites on the basis of the modern names of some villages. The editors of the inscriptions have identified some of the sites on the basis of the similarly in names, and the same methodology has been followed in this work to identify some more sites, both on the basis of similarity in names and the geographical location of the sites mentioned in the inscriptions, a method which is explained below.

The inscriptions mention a site called Valmīka – Tallavāṭaka. R. C. Majumdar, the editor of the *Epigraphia Indica,* says that this is to be identified with Talwara Deb, lying south of Narmada, 59 kms. south-east of Bagh (*EI* 15: 286-90). Since this is supposed to be in the division called 'Nagarīka – Pathaka' (Ramesh and Tiwari, 1991: 65, lines 2-5) and another inscription (*Ibid*: 41, lines 2-4) mentions a village called 'Cāravāhaka' lying in the same Nagarīka-Pathaka division, it follows that Cāravāhaka would be somewhere near Talwara Deb, although its exact location cannot be determined. These two villages, thus, have been marked in the same place on the map (Map 2). There is another territorial division called Dāsilakapallīpathaka, which has been identified (*EI* 37: 243-46) as lying south of Bagh, at a distance of 24 kms. It we accept this identification then all the villages mentioned in the inscriptions as lying in this division are to be located as somewhere close to Deswalia, even if we do not know their exact location (Map 2). Similarly, there is an important division called Udumbaragartta-Pathaka, referred to as lying on the southern bank of Narmada (Ramesh and Tiwari 1991: 33). It has been identified in this work as Ummeda, which lies on the southern-bank of Narmada, 29.5 kms. from Maheshwar. Nearby is a village called Nagajhiri, which may be identified with Nāgavardhanaka of the inscriptions (*Ibid*: 58, lines 3-4), which lies in Udumbaragartta. Hence, on the basis of both these places, other places referred to as lying in Udumbaragartta can be considered as lying near the two sites mentioned above. This is an example of how villages can be located on the basis of their geographical location, territorial units as mentioned above and on the basis of similarity in names and other sites identified.

Here, a special mention needs to be made of a group of modern villages, which are named as 'Brāhmaṇa-gāon', 'Brāhmaṇa-purī', etc. Although they are not mentioned in the inscriptions, they are located in the vicinity of the clusters of some of the tentatively identified sites. Thus, they may deserve a mention on the map, as in this predominantly tribal region, where modern sites have generally local names, the villages having such names as Brāhmaṇagāon or Brāhmaṇapurī are conspicuous and suggest a possible initial Brahmanical activity (Map 2).

The above can show that the methodology employed in identification of the sites and therefore, in reconstruction of a map of Valkhā gives us an idea of its extent and also, its location in relation to the major centres, the settlement pattern and possible expansion of settlements and inhabitation of new areas (suggesting an expansion of Valkhā territory through new settlements brought about by the grants) etc. The last two have been mentioned in the next chapter while discussing the socio-economic impacts of acculturation process in Valkhā.

As has been described earlier, apart from the inscriptions, works of art from the Bagh Caves form other major sources in this work. These works of art include the architecture, sculpture and the paintings. As not much of the sculptures and paintings have survived, part of our observations is based on the writings of the visitors to these caves during the colonial period. The earliest among them was Dr. Impey who visited the caves sometime in 1850s, and read a paper about them in 1854. This was published later in 1856 in the *Bombay Branch of the Royal Asiatic Society*. Many of his descriptions, which do not exist now in either stone or paint, are extremely useful to us. Later, Maj. C. E. Luard visited the caves about half a century later and published an article in the *Indian Antiguary* in 1910, along with illustrations. Although his article is largely a repetition of Dr. Impey, some of his illustrations are helpful, as has been shown in the chapter related to the works of art. Mukul Dey was the next to visit the caves in 1920s and published a travelogue in 1925, which provides some useful descriptions and illustrations.

In a major work, descriptions and illustrations of the sculptures, paintings and architecture with an attempt at interpretation are made, by John Marshall, Vogel and others, published in 1927. To this the present work has added information from M. D. Khare's work, Sandhya Pandey's illustrations published in 1991 and some observations made during my personal visit to the Caves.

In this study, an attempt has been made to study the works of art not merely from the viewpoint of their artistic expressions, but to relate these works to the information from the inscriptions. It has been said before that seeing the nature of the historical process going on here, the art and the acculturation process reflected in the grants can not be dissociated from each other, i.e., they have to be seen as complementary to each other. Just as the inscriptions provide us with evidence of the impact that Brahmanism had in the region, in the same way, the works of art provide us an insight into how Buddhism was interacting with the local culture, approximately at the same time, i.e., in the second and the third phases (AD 353-487) of the grants.

The architectural lay-out has been looked at from the functional point of view and to show the composition of the monk-body and the nature of practices followed by the monastic order. The sculptures have been studied to show how Buddhism underwent a change from *Hīnayāna* to *Mahāyāna*, assimilated and incorporated popular and local cults and experimented with the forms of deities which crystallised into the forms of Bodhisattvas in later periods. The mention of local cults is important here. Paintings have been studied to show how the artistic symbolism was used to show the stages of transformation that Buddhism underwent and the reasons behind the choice of certain *Jātaka* stories and how they were influenced by local elements.

The division of the chapters follows the main trends discussed in the first section of this chapter, keeping these trends in mind, the first chapter shows the processes of acculturation in Valkha region in three phases, both in the socio-economic and religious spheres. In order to see the other influences in the region, i.e. Buddhism and its composition, and how the local elements overshadowed by the Brahmanism were received by Buddhism, the second chapter has been constructed accordingly. Since this kind of study calls for further reflections on the complexities of the visual manifestations of the acculturation process, that last chapter attempts to show the possible linkages between the visual art and the more direct and authentic epigraphs.

The study of a region which has not been researched with indepth before is beset with many problems. The foremost of these is the fact that Valkha region remains unexcavated, and hence, any identification of sites, analysis etc., awaits confirmation through excavations in the area. Another problem is in the study of the works of art, most of which have vanished now. Although we have some illustrations and descriptions as described earlier, there is always a difference between an illustration of an existing work and a description. The surviving paintings are only in fragments, many figures having vanished. These obstruct the analytical process. The long panel of paintings in Cave 4 had an inscription painted underneath it, only one letter ('*Ka*') of which had survived by John Marshall's times. Had it survived, it would have given valuable information for analysis. However, it is lost to us forever, as is the date of the Bagh-Cave plate of Subandhu, thus necessitating a comparison between this and another dated plate of Subandhu for an estimation of it date.

As a result of the above fragmentary data, an attempt at drawing a correlation between the two facets of the influencing trends is extremely difficult – the correlation appears only when one leaves the plane of objectivity and looks beyond into the ideational plane. This will be evident in the last chapter where this method is employed, partly because of the fragmentary nature of the sources and the absence of excavation.

THE PROCESSES OF TRANSFORMATION – VALKHĀ'S CHANGING PROFILE (AD 358- 487)

Valkhā's development as a historical region would seem to fall under 3 phases in which the changes in its economy, society and religion are interrelated and complementary. The present study demarcates these three phases on the basis of both the epigraphic records registering grants and the works of art which appear as the visual – manifestations of the change. As a result one perceives an essentially non-Sanskritised region of the pre-Gupta period being transformed into a predominantly Brahmanised cultural region in the Gupta period with the earlier Buddhist forms continuing to be patronised in a significant way. The grants recovered from Valkhā region fall under six chiefs, from the year 38 (AD 358) to the year 167 (AD 487). A result of this accultration was the transformation of the agrarian structure of the region, as the land-grants given to Brāhmaṇas had the inevitable connotation of the intensification and the expansion of the agrarian structure. The grants also show that they were related to a polity different from an organised, complex administrative set-up, but show an emerging polity over time, perhaps, in an effort to keep pace with the growing outside influences and consequently a rapidly changing society in Valkhā.

As said earlier, on the basis of transformation taking place in Valkhā, the period of our study can be divided into broadly three phases – the first phase from the year 38 to the year 59 (AD 358 – 379), comprising of the reigns of a single ruler named Bhuluṇḍa, the second phase from the year 63 to the year 134 (AD 383-454), covering the reigns of four chiefs, Svāmidāsa, Rudradāsa, Bhaṭṭāraka and Nāgabhaṭṭa; and the third phase covering the period upto the year 167 (AD 487), the last date in this study and covered by the reign of Subandhu.

All the phases show remarkably different characteristics, showing the extent of change in society of Valkhā according to these influences, and at the same time of the external cultural forces themselves being oriented according to the social matrix of Valkhā, thus showing a cultural flux, i.e., the interaction of the local and external and cultural forces transforming both to form a new social matrix.

In the following sections, we deal with these three phases and so the basic trends in social and economic and religious sphere going on in Valkhā which changed its social structure. In essence, the changes are related to the broad or trend of an overall spread of the Sanskritic culture to the even smaller pockets of north India, during this period. Hence, the acculturation process evident in Valkhā should be seen in the context of this broader framework. The land-grants and their characteristics discussed below should also be seen in the context of the efforts of the Valkhā chiefs to emulate the Gupta period, who were their contemporaries and overlords, as discussed in the previous chapter.

(I)

The first phase, as stated above, covers the period 38 to the year 59 (AD 358-379), and coincides with the reign of the earliest ruler from copper plates, viz., Bhuluṇḍa. This is the period which shows what kind of local characteristics existed in Valkhā in socio-religious terms before an overpowering Brahmanical system engulfed the region.

Bhuluṇḍa's grants show a mixed-economy prevailing in the region i.e. parallel forms of economy-base existing along with the agrarian economy. Besides, this is the phase when the *Brahmadeyas* begin to appear in Valkhā region, although they are only four in number, other grants of Bhuluṇḍa being *Devāgrahāras*. Thus, the first phase of this study shows that the acculturation process to be discussed here was linked to the appearance of Brahmadeyas in Bhuluṇḍa's reign. It also shows that in the first phase, although the alternative economy-bases existed, agrarian structure was becoming relatively stronger even in this phase, although the process was accelerated only in the next phase. Thus, the emergence of Brāhmaṇas as a patronised group signified an instrumental development in the history of Valkhā.

The presence of economic-bases other than cultivation and their getting a space in the grants to either Brāhmaṇas or local deities during the time of Bhuluṇḍa is evident from at least three inscriptions. The first one of these mentions the grant by Bhuluṇḍa of three villages and a *carikā* to a local deity (Ramesh and Tiwari 1991: 20, line 6). Another inscription, again a *devāgrahāra*, records the grant of a villages and a 'Vāṭa-*Kaccha*' (*Ibid*: 22, line 5). The editors of the Bagh inscriptions have translated '*vāṭakaccha*' as 'marshy garden-land' (Ibid: 23). However, D.C. Sircar defines a '*Kaccha*' as a 'field bordering a stream, land near a well' (Sircar 1966: 137). Going by this definition, a '*vāṭakaccha*' should be interpreted as a garden lying in an area bordering on a stream, while *carikā* signifies a pastoral land. The third inscription in this sequence grants a piece of land alongwith the surrounding *kaccha* as a *Brahmedya* (Ramesh and Tiwari 1991: 63, line 4).

The granting of these alternative forms of economy bases e.g., pastoral land, garden land etc. shows that in the first phase in Valkhā, covering Bhuluṇḍa's reign, these kinds of lands still had importance, so much so that they were considered appropriate enough to be given away as grants by the ruler. This shows that although cultivation was important, these lands were also a part of the economic structure of Valkhā. As for the agrarian economy, we have evidence for Bhuluṇḍa's efforts to bring uncultivated land under cultivation and also to facilitate and intensify cultivation in the already cultivated areas.

Of special mention are two inscriptions from Bhuluṇḍa's reign, one of them is the grant of five villages alongwith a reservoir as a *devāgrahāra* (*Ibid*: 1, lines 2-6) and the other is the grant of three plots of land and a plot of waste-land (*Ibid*: 9, line 4), again as a *devāgrahāra*. The mention of a reservoir alongiwth five villages implies an attempt to facilitate the cultivation of the relatively large area of five villages. Incidentally, in the conventional list of people to whom the inscription is addressed, the word for cultivators does not exist. By contrast, in another inscription, the grant has been addressed to the '*kṛṣyamānāh*' (*Ibid*: 9, line 8) among others. This difference makes possible a suitable distinction between the two grants, while in one case, the absence of the world '*kṛṣyamānāh*' shows that probably cultivation was not a major feature of these villages and hence, the ruler's efforts to facilitate cultivation in these villages by granting a reservoir. In another case, the presence of the word '*kṛṣyamānāh*' and the fact that a waste-land has been granted along with the three plots of land (*Ibid*: 9, lines 2-6) which were cultivated, shows that cultivation was a major feature in these plots, which was used by the ruler to bring the waste-land under cultivation. Thus, in one case, Bhuluṇḍa tried to intensify agriculture, in another case, he brought an uncultivated piece of land under cultivation by granting it along with three cultivated plots.

There is another kind of evidence related to agrarian structure in Valkhā. The very first grant of Bhuluṇḍa is that of a village where "cultivation has terminated" (*Ibid*, Appendix I: 60, line 5). This villager "earlier belonged to the *agrahāra* of Ārya-Dharodhṛtaka" (*Ibid*: 60, line 2) and was regranted to seven Brāhmaṇas. These references show that the village had already existed as an *agrahāra* and belong to another person. It was regranted to another group of Brāhmaṇas as the cultivation had declined here, and Bhuluṇḍa wanted to revive it. This, apart from the agrarian planning of Bhuluṇḍa, also shows that the donee could enjoy the grant as long as he fulfilled the condition of *Brahmadeya*. However, if the cultivation declined or was neglected, the ruler could always regrant it to some other donee. Looking at these evidences, it seems that there were three basic trends going along with the land-grants of the first phase in terms of agrarian economy – (1) uncultivated areas were brought under cultivation along with other cultivated areas, (2) cultivation was intensified in the already cultivated areas and (3) the existence of the alternative forms of economy-bases was still an important feature of Valkhā, although they were getting integrated into an agrarian structure. Their mention as a part of the granted land shows that the Valkhā settlements needed these forms of land along with the cultivated tracts. Thus, we can see the beginning of a process of intensive agriculture in Bhuluṇḍa's period, which existed along with other forms of economy. Perhaps, the trend of *Brahmadeyas* had a crucial role to play in this process as is evident from the fact that a land was regranted to seven Brāhmaṇas in other to restart cultivation in this village.

Coming to the socio-religious aspects of Valkhā in the first phase, we can see that the beginning of the acculturation process are evident even in these areas, just as the emerging Brahmanisation in the region changes its economic structure, as shown above. The local socio-religious forms are strongly evident in the first phase, while the Sanskritic norms made an appearance, although not as strongly marked as in the second phase. Just as the Brahmanisation influenced the agrarian economy, it also influenced the society and religion of Valkhā, as will be evident in the second phase. Thus, the emergence of Brahmanical culture in the first phase as described below is an important feature in the history of Valkhā.

In the first phase, Valkhā was a society with many indigenous traits, along with the emergence of Brahmainsation of the region. It also showed a gradual development of administrative machinery and some migration of Brāhmaṇas from outside. As a result of these, there was an intermingling of various streams of belief-systems.

Out of the fifteen grants of Bhuluṇḍa, four are Brahmadeys**,** while the rest *devāgrahāras***.** In one case, an erstwhile *Brahmadeya* was regranted as a *devāgrahāra* to a local deity, showing the strong position this cult had in the society of Valkhā. The predominent number of *devāgrahāras*, mostly to local cult deities, shows that Valkhā society in the first phase of grants was under a strong influence of indigenous belief-systems, while the Sanskritic culture represented by the *Brahamadeyas* were just beginning to surface in this region.

Among the *Brahmadeyas,* the first grant of Bhuluṇḍa is socially important (*Ibid*, Appendix 1: 60). It is a *Brahmadeya* which grants a village to seven Brāhmaṇas of various *sagotras.* The village was erstwhile an *agrahāra* under the care of a person called Ārya-Dharodhṛtaka (*Ibid,* Appendix 1: 60, line 2). Another significant factor is that it had been granted in the year 38 (AD 358) and was recounted again in the year 47 (AD 367) at the request of the assembly of Brāhmaṇas (*Brāhmaṇapariṣad)* (*Ibid*: 61, line 9) and was engraved on the copper-plate. The above references show that the Brāhmaṇas were not really a new feature to the Valkhan society, as the mention of *Brāhmaṇapariṣad* shows, but their position here was not strengthened yet. This is evident from the fact that the verbal order regarding a *Brahmadeya* needed to be recounted nine years later at the request of the *Brāhmaṇapariṣad* on copper-plate. This might have been because of some obstructions in the enjoyment of the *Brahmadeya* by the seven donees, hence they requested through the *Brāhmaṇapariṣad* to make the order more permanent. This also reflects on the activities of the *Brāhmaṇapariṣad.* The existence of an active *Brāhmaṇapariṣad* and the fact that the donated village was an erstwhile *agrahāra,* shows that neither the feature of granting *agrahāras* nor the presence of Brāhmaṇas started with Bhuluṇḍa, they were already in existence by the time of Bhuluṇḍa (although we do not have any earlier records of them). The land already in the possession of Brāhmaṇas was now brought under the institutionalisation of the *agrahāra* system.

An attempt by Bhuluṇḍa to regrant a land earlier under the care of a person whose social group is not specified, as a *Brahmadeya* to another person with a specified *gotra* is seen in one of the grants. Here, it is mentioned that the land was attached to or under the care of Indrasena (*Indrasena-Pratyaya*) (*Ibid*: 15, line 4). It was regranted to 'Jayavardhana, the son of Bhaṭṭi Dāma of *Hārita Sagotra*' (*Ibid*: 15, line 3). It is striking that Indrasena's *gotra* is not mentioned, thus making it difficult to relate him to any particular group, while Jayavardhana belongs to *Hārita Sagotra* and gets the grant as a *Brahmadeyam* suggesting that he was a Brāhmaṇa. It is possible that earlier the land was under the care of a non-Brāhmaṇa and Bhuluṇḍa granted it to a Brāhmaṇa. The suffix '*Pratyaya*' attached to Indrasena to shows that the land was under his care, points to an important feature of land holdings in Valkhā – largely, the land was not under individual ownership but parts of land were managed by various individuals. *Brahmadeyas* were instrumental in bringing these lands under the holdings of Brāhmaṇas. However, these transfers might not have been permanent, as we have seen in the first grant that an *agrahāra* was regranted by Bhuluṇḍa to 7 donees. Hence, the *Brahmadeyas* of the first phase made some changes in the indigenous concepts of land-holdings, but the ultimate power rested with the ruler to decide who should hold the land.

As mentioned earlier, there is some evidence that Bhuluṇḍa made some attempts to settle some Brāhmaṇas who came from outside in his chiefdom. His grant given in the year 56 (AD 376) (*Ibid*: 17, line 3) mentions the grant of a village to one 'Brāhmaṇa Dakkanna' of *Bhāradvāja Sagotra*. His name probably indicates his affiliation with Deccan or further south. However, merely on the basis of his name, it is not possible to say much about his origins as the charter does not mention his migration from anywhere. The use of such a name however, certainly shows Valkhā's connection with the southern regions.

The last one of the *Brahmadeyas* granted by Bhuluṇḍa in the year 57 (AD 377), gives evidence of not only the transferring of land-holding from a non-Brāhmaṇa to a Brāhmaṇa, but also of the fact that not only the ruler donated a land, but his subjects did so too; it is mentioned that a piece of land along with the surrounding *kaccha* was under the care of a person called Khuddataka ('Khuddataka-pratyaya') (*Ibid*: 63, lines 2-6), which was granted to a Brāhmaṇa Kuśāraka of *Bhāradvāja sagotra* at the request of Āṣāḍhanandī (*Ibid*: 63, line 3). The transfer of land from the care of a non-Brāhmaṇa (as the name 'Khuddataka' suggests) to a Brāhmaṇa has been discussed earlier. Here, this grant shows that sometimes the donor was not the ruler but another person (Āśāḍhanandī in this case), who requested the ruler to make the grant ('*vijñapya*'). This again shows that ultimately it was the ruler who decided about land-donations and if anyone wanted to make a grant, he or she had to request the ruler regarding it. This is also evident form several *Devāgrahāras* to be discussed later in which a woman called Bhojikā Bhaṭṭa Bandhulā requested Bhuluṇḍa to grant some land to a local deity.

The above instances of the *Brahmadeyas* show the main features of the society of Valkhā in the first phase. They show that the indigenous concepts of land-holdings of Valkhā underwent a change under the influence of Brahmadeyas, although only to some extent. They also show that there was some effort by Bhuluṇḍa to settle Brāhmaṇas, as some pieces of land were transferred from non- Brāhmaṇas to Brāhmaṇas. Apart from this, the Brāhmaṇas were not a new feature in Valkhā during this time, but were not a strongly-felt authority yet. They were only beginning to show their presence felt in the first phase. The emerging new forms of agrarian economy discussed earlier should be seen in conjunction with these factors.

This feature of a strong presence of the indigenous structure, with the surfacing traits of Brahmanism in the first phase is also seen in the nature of inscriptions themselves. As stated earlier, only 4 out of 15 grants of Bhuluṇḍa are Brahmadeyas, the rest are all *Devāgrahāras* out of which, only one grant gives land to a Brahmanical deity, the rest grant land to the deities of local cults. Thus, first phase shows the beginnings of trends which brought about the acculturation in Valkhā, although the indigenous trends were still very strong. The only *Devāgrahāras*, showing brahmanical influence is an early grant of Bhuluṇḍa, of the year 47 (AD 367), and records the grant of 5 villages and a water reservoir, for the performance of *Bali, cāru* and *sattra* for Viṣṇu who is described as eight-armed and carrying various weapons in these arms (*Ibid*: 1-2). This grant is unusual in its format, as apart from its conventional passages referring to the grant, it contains a long passage describing the traits of Viṣṇu.

The Puranic influence in this grant is proved from the fact that this descriptive passage referring to Viṣṇu contains all the Puranic references of Viṣṇu's characteristics e.g., his weapons, his bed of milky ocean, lotus arising from his navel etc. and also indicates his four incarnations – those of Vāmana, Kṛṣṇa, Rāma and Varāha. Here, it is worth nothing that these incarnations are not mentioned by name, but Viṣṇu is referred to as the deity who broke the pride of Bali, Rāvaṇa, Kansa, Cāṇūra, Śiśupāla etc. Only Varāha is mentioned by name (*Ibid*: 1-2, lines 1-5).

Apart from these references, Viṣṇu is also referred to as the deity who broke the pride of

Naraka and Naumci (*Ibid*: 1-2, line 3). Here, it is to be noted that the Puranic version describes Kṛṣṇa (not Viṣṇu) as Narakāri, Narakajit etc. Also, Namuci was an *Asura* slain by Indra, not by Visnu or his incarnations (Apte 1988: 280). Moreover, the charter ends by referring to Bhuluṇḍa as the devotee/servant of Nārāyaṇa ("*Nārāyaṇadāsa*") (Ramesh and Tiwari 1991: 2, line 9).

The above references show that there was a congruity between the religious and the socio-economic aspects of the first phase of Valkhā as described earlier. This grant to a Brahmanical deity shows that Brahmanism was still at a preliminary stage of creating an impact in Valkhā, which largely followed the local cults, as will be shown later. This impact on Valkhā is shown by this inscription. While the description of Viṣṇu follows the Brahmanical precepts closely, the identities between Viṣṇu, his incarnations, Indra and the local deity Nārāyaṇadeva are blurred, as shown by the descriptions (for a discussion on the folk/tribal nature of the deity called Nārāyaṇa, see Jayaswal 1980: 32-35). Thus, the inscription shows that the Brahmanical religion was well accepted in Valkhā and even received patronage through this grant. This inscription also shows that this is the point of time when there was no clear demarcation left between Viṣṇu, the Brahmanical deity and Nārāyaṇa, the popular cult deity of Valkhā and elsewhere. Thus, two later grants by Bhuluṇḍa to Nārāyaṇa might well be taken as grants to brahmanical religion as well as the local cult, thus giving space to the Brahmanical religion through these *devāgrahāras*. In this sense, we can say that the introduction of the Brahmanical religion in Valkhā brought the local cults into a complex interaction with this new element and helped in the acculturation process in the religious field.

Coming to the local cults present in Valkhā which got royal patronage in the first phase, apart from the reference to the *devāgrahāras* granted to Nārāyaṇa as stated above, we have references to the mother-goddesses, Mahāsenadeva and an ancestral deity, Bappa-Piśāca-deva. *Devāgrahāras* to these form the bulk of the grants of Bhuluṇḍa. We should, rather than seeing them as clearly demarcated cults, see them as inter-allied cults, or perhaps, as the vehicle of the local belief-system of Valkhā which carried the pantheon of these deities. The reason for these will be clear from the discussion that follows.

The mother-goddesses or 'Bhagvatīs' were probably local village deities which got patronage during the first phase of these grants – in one case, they were installed by the ruler (Ramesh and Tiwari 1991: 4, line 3) and in another case they were installed by Pāśupatācārya Bhagavat Lokodadhi (*Ibid*: 22, line 3). Grants were given in both cases by Bhuluṇḍa. The installation of Bhagavatīs by a Pāśupatācārya is important. The inscription also refers to the Pāśupatas who were associated with the temple and who were enjoined by the ruler to endorse the grant in accordance with the rules of *devāgrahāras* (*Ibid*: 22, lines 7-8). This kind of reference shows that Bhagvatīs were a part of the Pāśupata pantheon. This is also reflected in the name of the Pāśupatācārya which includes the epithet '*Bhagavat*'. The use of this epithet along with 'Pāśupatācārya' shows that the two terms were interrelated through religion. Here, *Bhagavat* seems to have originated from 'Bhagavatī'. Thus, the Pāśupatācārya was both a devotee of the *Pāśupata* sect and of Bhagavatī.

The interaction between various cults/ sects is also seen from the fact that Pāśupatas are referred to as associated with a shrine of Mahāsenadeva, which received a grant from Bhuluṇḍa, Nārāyaṇadeva and Bappa-Piśāca-deva who was a major deity receiving patronage from Bhuluṇḍa. It is worth noticing that Mahāsenadeva was an epithet of Kārttikyea in the Brahmanical religion (Apte 1988: 432).

A special reference needs to be made to Bappa-Piśāca-deva who received four grants in the first phase and who seems to have been a major local deity of Valkhā during the first phase. The editors of the Bagh Inscriptions have mentioned that the name of the deity suggests either the prevalence of the worship of spirits in this tribal region, or the worship of an ancestor who met with an unnatural death (Ramesh and Tiwari 1991: Introduction, xiii-xiv). The shrine of this deity was installed at the capital of Valkhā itself by a woman called Bhojikā-Bhaṭṭa-Bandhulā who requested the ruler to grant several *devāgrahāras* to this deity. The strong following of this cult is evident from the fact that the last grant of Bhuluṇḍa in the year 59 (AD 379) concludes the first phase of these characters from Valkhā, by granting two vilalges in the *'Narmadā-para-pāra-viṣaya*, to a shrine of Bapa-Piśāca-deva installed in this *viṣaya* itself. Thus, by the end of the first phase, this cult had spread south of Narmada. As the very first grant of Bhuluṇḍa was located on the southern bank of Narmada, it may be said that the expansion of the Valkhā settlements had started in the very beginning of Bhuluṇḍa's reign. However, the installation of their ancestral deity south of Narmada through the last inscription of Bhuluṇḍa may show that this expansion had become full-fledged by this time, and an agrarian-base in this visays was well established. Incidentally, this grant was made at the request of not Bhojikā, but a person called Iṇṇapada (*Ibid*: 28, lines 4-5). This name clearly suggests the non-Brahmanical base of this cult.

Another important point suggesting not only a strong following of this cult in the first phase, but also a prominent position of the popular belief-systems of Valkhā during the first phase is that one of the villages called Jayasenānaka (not identfied) was an erstwhile *Brahmadeya,* entrusted with Agnīśvaraka (*"Pūrva-Brahmadeya - Kṣetram - Agnīśvaraka - Pratyaya"*) (*Ibid*: 28, lines 4-5) which was regranted as devāgrahāra to Bappa- Piśāca-deva. Thus, the popular belief-system was so strong in the first phase that the ruler could go to the extent of converting an erstwhile *Brahmadeya* into a *devāgrahāra* to a local deity. This also shows the not so strong position of Brahmanism in the first phase, as has been discussed earlier.

Another feature that emerges from the references to this local deity is that of the association of a woman (Bhojikā-Bhaṭṭa-Bandhulā) with this cult and the *devāgrahāra* related to this deity. It shows that the pre-Brahmanised society of Valkhā was a society which gave a visible space to women, who could perpetuate a cult-worship and even approach the ruler to grant *devāgrahāras* to the cult deity. This kind of a system in which women had access to a visible space was overshadowed in the second phase of the acculturation process in Valkhā. The cult of mother-goddesses' worship is also perhaps indirectly related to giving a defined or prominent status to the feminine, among other things. In this sense, these two references – of Bhojikā and of mother-goddesses, point towards the same thing.

The interrelation between various cults discussed earlier is also obvious from a phraseology used in the grants related to the ancestral deity. Out of four, the earlier two grants, both from the year 54 (AD 374), mention in the end that the "grant is to be administered by the devotees of the *Bhāgavat"* (*"Bhāgavat-śiṣṭaih adhikṛtam"*) (*Ibid*: 11, line 8; 13, line 8). The editors of this board have interpreted this term as devotees of Lord Nārāyaṇa (*Ibid*: 12, 14). However, it may be recalled here that the Pāśupatācārya mentioned earlier is also referred as to as *'Bhāgavat'*, owing to his association with Bhagavatī worship. Taking this in conjunction with the fact that *Nārāyaṇa-bali* is performed for a person meeting with an unnatural death (Jaiswal 1980: 32-34), it can be said that some aspect of *Nārāyaṇa-bali* or a likewise ritual was involved with the worship of Bappa-Piśāca-deva, therefore, the administration of the grant by the *'Bhagavat-śiṣyas'*. Also, it can be said that the cult of Nārāyaṇa, Paśupati, Bhagavatī and Bappa-Piśāca-Deva were inter-allied cults and there was no strict demarcation between their followers and officiating devotees cultwise – the devotees of one deity could very well be the devotee of another deity as well as the officiating 'priest' of the ritual involved with one cult could also administer the affairs of another cult. Thus, most probably, these deities represented the pantheon of the religious belief-system of Valkhā, and should not be seen as the deities of distinct cults.

These shrines, apart from the Pāśupatas and the *Bhagavat-śiṣṭas*, also associated with them *mantra gaṇācārayas, Ārya-Cokas* (Ramesh and Tiwari 1991: 7, line 6), *Ācāryas (Ibid*: 28, line 6)**,** *Devakīya Karṣakah* (*Ibid*: 6, line 5)**,** *devaprāsādakah* (*Ibid*: 11, line 6), *Devakarmmāntika Ācārya* (Ibid: 29, line 7) and *Deva-Karmmāntikas*, (both mentioned together in the last grant of Bhuluṇḍa, granted to Bappa-Piśāca-Deva seem to be the temple-instructions of the religious precepts and temple priest respectively) (*Ibid*: 29, line 7). This also shows that the particular shrine of Bappa-Piśāca-Deva was larger than the other shrines, since it needed additional groups of priests.

The mention of *Ārya-Cokas* is the only epigraphical reference to this sect according to the editors (*Ibid*: Introduction, xiv). They are a *Bhāgavata* sect, depicted in the *Cāturbhāṇī* as believing in hypocrisy and practices like untouchability and therefore, ridiculed (Chandra 1959: 21-23). Incidentally, in the present inscription, they are associated with the temple of Nārāyaṇadeva. Thus, their association with the *Bhāgavata* sect is quite likely.

Among the people engaged in rendering services to the temples, '*Devakīya karṣakaha*' are referred to as 'tilling the land and sowing the seeds' (Ramesh and Tiwari 1991: 6, line 5), suggesting that the temple authorities had regular tillers to work on the land of the temple – thus, temple grants were becoming more or less institutionalised, although this process was still in an initial stage. *Deva-Prāsādakahas* are engaged in providing incense, garlands, sandal paste etc. – i.e. generally they were engaged in the temple activities related to worship. Thus, they seem to have been temple-servants.

A constant occurrence in association with all the devagraharas is the reference to the offering of *bali*, *cāru* and *sattra*. This terminology shows the kind of rituals which were observed along with the worship of the deities. D. C. Sircar explains these terms as offerings included in five *Mahāyajñas* essential for the Brāhmaṇas. *Bali* was the offering of flowers, fruits uncooked rice etc. (Sircar 1966: 45). *Cāru* was the offering to manes or ancestors (*Ibid*: 67) while *sattra* was a charitable feeding house (*Ibid*: 306). However, looking at the variety in the pantheon worshipped in Valkhā, they can not be taken in the restricted context of belonging to the five *Mahāyajñas* of Brāhmaṇas. Rather, offerings explained above show the kind of ritual system followed by the people of Valkhā, which later evolved into the Brahmanical *Mahāyajñas*, as reflected in the second phase to be discussed later. Thus, they reflect the popular origins of these *Mahāyajñas*. This system embedded in the popular stratum is also reflected in the terms '*mantragaṇācāryas*, indicating some form of incantation accompanying these rituals.

The above analysis shows, as stated earlier, that in the first phase, the Valkhā society was predominantly based on the popular belief-systems, as reflected in the study on the society and religion of Valkhā. Brahmanism started emerging as a visible force in this period, but it was only in the initial stage of emergence. The economy was a mixed one, although cultivation was becoming intensified by the efforts of the ruler. Local cults were more forceful than the Brahmanical influence, although the latter also had started getting patronage from the ruler. There were certain features in Valkhā society e.g., popular cults, women getting a space in the patronage system, ritual system based in the popular nature etc., which were prominent in this phase, but were to get overshadowed in the next phase, as will be shown later. Patronage to the temple was one of these, which did not get patronage in the next phase.

Thus, the first phase gives us a picture of what pre-acculturated Valkhā was like, and what features of acculturation emerged in the first phase. The second phase can show us in what forms these features of acculturation became strong and also, in some case, how they incorporated the local features in their system.

(II)

The first phase of emergent Brahmanism had brought about an attempt by the chief to intensify cultivation in Valkhā and to settle land along the southern bank of the Narmada, as was shown in the earlier section. The second phase to be discussed here shows an advanced stage of this acculturation process ad its impact on socio-religious and agrarian systems. We find that many features which were characteristic of the first phase stopped finding a mention in the grants of the second phase, while the traits of acculturation process became prominent and absolutely dominated the grants of this phase. This also affected the agrarian structure of Valkhā, as will be shown below.

The main trends in the agrarian economy, exercised by the four chief of this phase from the year 63 to the year 134 (AD 383 to 454), in order to emulate the 'high-culture' of Brahmanical society included several features which are normally associated with a Brahmanised socio-economic structure. These include, among other things, a uniformity in the format of the grants and in contents, as against the grants of Bhuluṇḍa, which showed a diversity in the forms of land granted, to various kinds of donees etc. the grants of the second phase are all *Brahmadeyas*, which record the grant of generally a single village or a single piece of land to a Brāhmaṇa or a group of Brāhmaṇas.

The diversity in the kind of Bhuluṇḍa's grants can be explained in terms of his efforts to patronise the indigenous elements, while giving space to the elements of influence at the same time. In agrarian terms, this meant donating various kinds of land to Brāhmaṇas or to the shrines of local cults, as well as granting pure Brahmadeya lands for intensification of agriculture and for the expansion of settlements south of Narmada. Once all this was achieved, a form of uniformity was established in the kinds of grants and also, the Brāhmaṇa donees took a prominent place in the second phase. The grant of single villages/plots in the second phase reflects intensified agrarian economy, so a plot of land was considered enough as a grant, while in the first phase, several villages or a village with several plots were granted together by Bhuluṇḍa, showing that agrarian economy was not so well intensified and also, that Bhuluṇḍa wanted to bring additional land under cultivation.

Several other features in the agrarian economy of the second phase indicate an attempt by the rulers to settle deserted and uninhabited land, some evidence for the expansion of Valkhan territory south of Narmada, experimentation with paddy cultivation in one instance and a gradually evolving economic apparatus as the mention of the granting the right to collect revenue appears in one grant, these will be discussed below, we should remember that the increasing Brahmanisation of the region was instrumental in the emergence of this kind of economic apparatus in Valkhā.

As stated above, the second phase-rulers made some effort to settle uninhabited land and as a result, the Valkhan settlement-area expanded south of the Narmada. This was an advance over the previous phase, in which lands were donated on the southern bank of Narmada. We have evidence regarding this from four records from the second phase, inscribed in close proximity of time. Three inscriptions out of these, one from the year 69 AD 386) of Svāmidāsa, and two from the year 69 (AD 386) of Rudradāsa refer to a territorial division called Navarāṣṭraka' or Navarāṣṭrakapathaka lying south of Narmada, while one inscription of the year 67 (AD 387) of Rudradāsa refers to a '*Śūnya-grāmakam*'. The term 'Navarāṣṭraka' connotes the sense of a territorial division newly settled, lying south of Narmada, as mentioned earlier. It seems that after grants were given along the southern bank of Narmada, some uninhabited area left in between clusters of settlements was settled by the rulers and given the name 'Navarāṣṭraka' (Map 2) after it developed into a *rāṣṭra*.

There are several grants given in the 'Navarāṣṭraka' or pathaka of the same name (Ramesh and Tiwari 1991: 39, line 3; Map 2). Two of these villages have been granted to *Cāturvaidya* Brāhmaṇas who are residents of the centre and are asked to inhabit ('*Samāvāsayatah*') these villages, as also is the Brāhmaṇa Dantika, who is also granted a village in this *rāṣṭra*. Thus, there is clear evidence that in the second phase effort was made by the rulers to inhabit and settle erstwhile uninhibited land and they sent the *Cāturvaidya* Brāhmaṇas from the centre and other Brāhmaṇas in other cases for this purposes.

The *Śūnya-grāmakam* referred to above was also granted as a Brahmadeya and the donee was asked to 'cultivate it, get it cultivated and to settle it' (*Ibid:* lines 5-6, "*Bhuñjatah, kṛṣatah, kṛṣāpayatah, Samāvāsayatah*; the interpretation of the terms '*samāvāsayatah*' has been left by the translators).

Here again, the word *Samāvāsyatah* has been used, as in the three grants discussed above. Besides, the editors of this inscription have translated the term *Śūnya-grāmakam* as an 'uninhabited village' (*Ibid*: 70, lines 2-5). If this interpretation is correct, then it shows that this was another effort by Rudradāsa to settle an uninhibited villages, (this time in Dāsilakapalli pathaka), just as in the case of settlement of the Navarāṣṭraka-pathaka.

The features of the experimentation of paddy cultivation and the emergence of an infra-structure based on revenue-collection are evident from an inscription of the year 102 (AD 422) of Bhaṭṭāraka, Rudradāsa's successor (*Ibid*: 52). This shows that under the influence of the acculturation process, there was an effort by the rulers in the second-phase not only to intensify cultivation, but also to patronise the cultivation of paddy, which needs water resources and also organisation of labour. We do not know what was cultivated in Valkhā in the earlier period, as there is no reference to the crops cultivated, but the fact that the paddy fields get a mention in this grant and that *udranga*-revenue goes along with them, shows that it was an important step in the second phase; we do not have a mention of this kind in any other grant. This inscription shows that the political and economic machinery of Valkhā had evolved considerably from Bhuluṇḍa's time, since by AD 422 a Brāhmaṇa was granted the right to collect *udranga* (*Ibid*: 52, lines 4-5), (revenue) and there was sufficient labour organisation machinery at least in this instance to introduce paddy-cultivation. However, it is worth-noticing that these references are not repeated in the second phase at least, the subsequent grant reverting back to the older form of granting a piece of land or a village without any revenue rights whatsoever. Thus, it can be said that this grant shows a new experimentation in the second stage by Valkhā, an advance on the efforts of the previous phase to intensity cultivation and also, it shows an evolution of the administrative machinery regarding revenue. We don't know whether udranga existed earlier, but it had evolved as significant revenue by the time of this grant i.e. AD 422.

Thus, we can see that the agrarian economy shows an advance over the last phase here. There is an effort to expand the settled area of Valkhā, beyond the southern bank of Narmada referred to in the first phase, and to introduce probably new modes of cultivation of a new crop and also the introduction of revenue collection rights in the grant system, perhaps brought about by the increased yield of revenue form this area. The efforts to expand and settle new areas as also to improve cultivation may be linked to the topography of the region, which is not very fertile, except for the bank of Narmada. Thus, an evolving chiefdom needed additional revenue and surplus food, and therefore employed the Brahmanisation – factor in the first phase to strengthen its grounds of agrarian economy. An increase in population may also be a reason for the expansion of settled area and of cultivation. Also, the growing influx of Brāhmaṇas who sought patronage had to be settled somewhere. The sudden emergence of *Cāturvaidyas* in this phase suggests that either they migrated from outside or the existing Brāhmaṇas had consolidated themselves in leading groups of *Cāturvaidya*. However, we do not have a direct evidence for these factors – they are largely inferred. In any case, the economy of second phase definitely shows an advance over that of the last phase and Brāhmaṇas played a significant role in this transformation.

In socio-religious sphere too, we see an increasing influence of Brahmanism on Valkhā in the second phase. This accelerated the acculturation process which had emerged in the first phase. We see the impact of this influence on the social structure as well as references to the religious rituals etc. Not only is the Brahmanical influence seen to increase in this phase, but the Brāhmaṇa-community also is well established and more differentiated as compared to the previous phase. The increasing influence of Brāhmaṇas is seen from the fact that certain land-holdings were taken from non-Brāhmaṇas, often groups belonging to the lower strata of society and donated to Brāhmaṇas. This is different from such transfers discussed in the first phase, since the social-group affiliations of people from whom the land was transferred to Brāhmaṇas in the first phase are not clearly mentioned. In contrast, in the second phase these affiliations are clearly mentioned. Hence, it also shows that apart from the Brahmanical influences, social hierarchy in the second phase was more clearly established. Another feature is the emergence of the groups of *Cāturvaidyas,* perhaps an influential social group. As discussed in the section on economy, they helped in the expansion of the settled area of Valkhā. Their reference also helps us to understand a grater differential status of Brāhmaṇas as will be discussed later.

The increasing Brahmanical influence over the region also points toward a greater homogenisation of the cultural-matrix of the region. We no longer find a mention of the varied popular cults which were prominent in the first phase. The only such reference is that of a forest deity, and in an indirect manner. This shows that the popular cults took a backstage in the second phase. The local ritual system also underwent a transformation under the influence of Brahamanism and was incorporated in the Brahmanical order to serve the needs of this new dominant trend. Thus, what was only surfacing as a major influence in the first phase became a prominent feature in the second phase.

The evidence of the transfer of land-holdings from a non-Brāhmaṇa to a Brāhmaṇa comes from two grants of the year 67 (AD 387), one by Svamidāsa and the other by Rudradāsa. The former mentions the donation of a *Brahmadeya* to a 'Muṇḍā Brāhmaṇa', this land erstwhile being under the care of one 'Āryya-Vaṇijaka' (*Ibid*: 65, lines 3-4). The word *vaṇijaka* suggests his origin in the trading group, while the Brāhmaṇa's name suggests his possible upward social mobility from the Muṇḍas. The second grant records the donation of a field, like in the former inscription, which was under the care of a potter 'Ārya-dāsa' ('*kumbhakāra-ārya-dāsapratyaya*') (*Ibid*: 67, lines 3-4) to a Brāhmaṇa called H*ū*ṇāḍhyaka. The introduction of the Brāhmaṇas in a non-Brāhmaṇa area is also somewhat related to this feature described above. This is evident from an inscription of Svāmidāsa, of the year 65 (AD 385), by which a plot is granted to Matujja of *Kāśyapa sagotra,* which lies in a village called 'Lohakārapallikā', literally, a hamlet of iron-smiths (*Ibid*: 37, lines 3-4). Thus, not only was the land erstwhile under the care of non-Brāhmaṇas given to Brāhmaṇas, the latter were also introduced in an erstwhile non-Brahamanical area. Thus, we see a strong tendency to brahmanise the region by the rulers in the second phase.

That this tendency not only brought the Valkhan territory under an acculturation process but also strengthened the position of the Brāhmaṇas is seen from the fact that as many as seven grants in the second phase are given to the Ārya-Cāturvaidays of the cetnre, who were probably a dominant group of Brāhmaṇas. Their association with the expansion of settlements has been discussed earlier. Their sudden emergence is a remarkable thing, as nothing is mentioned regarding where they came from. There can be two possibilities regarding their appearance in the second phase – either they, in a group, migrated from somewhere else to Valkhā and received patronage from the chiefs and resided at the centre, or the influential Brāhmaṇa families of the first phase had aligned themselves in a *Cāturvaidaya* group by the second phase. In this context, the reference to a 'Brāhmaṇa-*pariṣad*' in the very first grant of Bhuluṇḍa is worth recalling. However, in the absence of any reference to their origin, nothing much can be said. Whatever may be the case, it is clear that they were an influential group, perhaps more influential than even other Brāhmaṇas. This is shown by the fact that almost all the chiefs from the second phase donated land to them – total seven in number, covering a period from the year 63 (AD 383) to the year 134 (AD 454), or the whole of the second phase. Thus, we can see that in the second phase, there was not only a social hierarchy established between Brāhmaṇas and other social group, but there was a hierarchy evident even amongst the Brāhmaṇas. This is certainly an advance over the first phase, where there was visible differentiation only among the Brāhmaṇas and others.

That the *Cāturvaidyas* had attained a greater stage of differentiation than other Brāhmaṇas is also evident from the fact that they are referred to as belonging to various *gotras* and *caraṇas* (although the specific *gotras* and *caraṇas* are not mentioned), while the other Brāhmaṇas are identified with only a *sagotra,* suggesting that they were lesser differentiated than the *Cāturvaidyas.* This again shows that Brāhmaṇas had evolved from the first phase, where there are no *Cāturvaidyas,* Brāhmaṇas are identified with only sagotras and no *caraṇas.* However, it is to be noted that although a reference to *caraṇas* emerges in the second phase, the names of *caraṇas* do not come down to us, and the stage of differentiation of Brāhmaṇas in the second phase has not reached a stage where their *śākhās* are mentioned. Thus, they are still in a process of differentiation.

As mentioned earlier, the excessive acculturation of the area led to the subordination of the popular cults as they cease to get royal patronage absolutely. However, that these cults still existed to some extent, is evident from an indirect reference to a possible cult of a forest-deity in the second phase. In the earlier stage of the second phase, in the year 65 (AD 383), there is a reference to 'Vanavāsin*ī*' while defining the location of a *Brahmadeya* which lay 'north-west to Vanavāsin*ī*' (*Ibid*: 35, lines 3-4). The editors of the inscriptions have taken this term to be a territorial division (*Ibid*: Introduction, xx). However, the reference suggests that it was a shrine of a forest-deity lying on the outskirts of a village, or a village named after a forest-deity. Whatever be the case, the cult of a forest-deity is definitely evident in the origin of this name. The indirect reference to it and also, no *devāgrahāra* to a popular cult in this period show that the emergence and the strengthening of Brahmanism gave a setback to the popular cults in this region in the second phase.

This growing influence not only suppressed the popular cults, it also incorporated the local ritual – system and transformed them in order to suit the needs of the Brahmanical religion. In the last grant of the second phase, in the year 134 (AD 454), to Ārya-Cāturvaidya a *Brahmadeya* is donated for the observance of *Bali*, *Cāru*, and *Vaiśvadeva* offerings (*Ibid*: 58, line 6). This shows a marked departure from the *devāgrahāras* of the first phase, where land was granted for '*Bali*, *Cāru* and *Sattra* rites, which reflected the ritual-system of the popular-worship. The substitution of the terms *sattra* in favour of '*Vaiśvadeva*' in the second phase is significant. D. C. Sircar explains *Vaiśvadeva'* as offerings to gods, i.e., one of the five *Mahāyajñas* performed by Brāhmaṇas (Sircar 1966: 359). The fact that the grant has been given to Ārya-Cāturvaidyas shows that the phrase '*Bali-Cāru-Vaiśvadeva*' had assumed the meaning of *Mahāyajñas* by AD 454 in Valkhā, transcending its popular origins from the first phase. Thus, a ritual system had been accommodated by the Brahmanical order to perpetuate itself.

The above discussion shows that the emerging trends of acculturation of phase I had become a dominant trend by Phase II, so much so that there was no legitimation left for the popular-systems. We see that, as a result of growing Brahmanism and perhaps a need felt for intensification of agriculture because of the aridness of much of Valkhā (or perhaps because it was forested), there was an attempt to not only intensify agriculture but also experimentation with paddy-cultivation. We also see the revenue-system becoming strong in this phase.

The socio-religious picture shows a complete dominance of the Brahmanical order. We get this reading not only from what is evident, but also from what is not evident. For example, the visible-space given to women and popular cults in the first phase is completely overshadowed, showing the impact of the dominance of Brahmanism. It does not mean that these cults did not exist in the second phase; it simply means that they were not considered important enough to be patronised. A parallel to this can be seen in the area of land-grant. In contrast to the first phase, when pasture-land, garden-land etc. were donated along with the cultivated land, in the second phase, there is no mention of these forms of land. They must have existed even in the second phase, since a settlement needs these types of land along with cultivated land, but it was not considered appropriate enough to grant such lands in the second phase. Thus, to some extent, acculturation had changed the perception of the people in the second phase.

Apart from the dominant Brahamanisation, we also see the emergence of various social groups not mentioned in the first phase, pointing towards a greater differentiation of the society, and also of the Brāhmaṇa community in the second phase. Thus, we can see that the acculturation process in Valkha had created a strong impact on the region by the end of second phase.

In the next section, we will see not only the emergence of Brahmanisation in its full-fledged form, but also, the prevalence of a new influence on the region which formed the third dimension of social transformation of Valkhā.

(III)

This phase, upto the year 167 (AD 487), comprises of only two grants, but they are extremely important, as they give information about the culmination-phase of acculturation in Valkhā, and also about the prevalence of a new influence over Valkhan society i.e. that of Buddhism. We have reasons to believe that Buddhism was introduced in Valkhā in late 5th century AD or in early 5th century AD (or perhaps even earlier) i.e., sometime in the second phase, when Brahmanism was a strong force. Thus, it shows that the centrestage in the second phase was shared by both sects equally, and this continued into the third phase. Certain features of the grants of this phase show that this co-existence of the two major sects in Valkhā led to a religious complexity in which Brahmanism affected the Buddhist grant.

The grants of this phase show that Valkhā attained an advanced state of administrative machinery, and a stronger polity in third phase. The social differentiation was also an advance over the last stage. Besides, Buddhism had begun to show its impact in this phase. It is worth noticing that Buddhism had existed here even in the second phase but did not receive a mention from the rulers of Valkhā, it made a strong impact only in the third phase. Perhaps, the changed status of Valkhā and its centre in the third phase had something to do with it.

Between the last inscription of the second phase (AD 454) and the first dated inscription of the third phase (AD 487), there is a gap of 33 years during which no inscription is available to us. When we get inscriptions again in AD 487, there is a marked change in the political status of Valkhā. Firstly, the grants are issued not from Valkhā as was the practice in earlier two phases, but from Māhiṣmatī. Secondly, the ruler of the third phase viz., Subandhu, does not pay obeisance to Gupta rulers as do the rulers of the first two phases. This shows that the hiatus of 33 years was a period of political disturbance, and when the political situation became stable again, the position of Valkhā had changed. Bagh had lost its political importance, the base had shifted from Bagh to Māhiṣmatī (i.e., present Maheshwar) and the chiefdom of Valkhā had come under a more powerful ruler, who did not acknowledge the suzerainty of any overload. Here, it should be noted that Subandhu was contemporary of Budhagupta, and studies show that in the last decades of 5th century AD, Budhagupta's empire included the land from eastern Mālava to northern Bengal and from Kali Nadi to Ganga. Thus, his kingdom comprised of North Bengal, Bihar, Eastern Uttar Pradesh and Eastern Mālava (Gupta 1974: 353). Here it is important to know that only Eastern Mālava is listed as under the control of Budhagupta and not Western Mālava, where the area of this study lies. Moreover, it is acknowledged by scholars that during this period the power of the Guptas was beginning to decline and many erstwhile feudatories and other local chiefs including Subandhu made no reference to any Gupta sovereign (*Ibid*: 353-354). Hence, we can safely say that Subandhu who ruled from Māhiṣmatī over the erstwhile Valkhā cheifdom was more or less an independent ruler and any allegiance which he had to the Guptas was nominal.

The above is true of the political independence of the Māhiṣmatī ruler and Valkhā territory. However, cultural and religious influences of Budhagutpa over Subandhu can not be denied. Rather, it explains Subandhu's patronage to the Bagh caves partly, as Budhagupta is also known to be a patron of Buddhism. Thus, the emulation tendency of the Valkhā rulers takes a different form in the third phase – in earlier phase they supported Brahmanical culture, while in this phase it led to a patronage of Buddhism, apart from usual patronage to Brahmanism.

Continuing the discussion on economic front from the earlier two phases, it is seen that Subandhu's grant to Bagh caves (identified by the editors as '*Kalāyana-Vihāra*' of the grant) includes the right to collect udranga and *Uparaikara* taxes, apart from the donation of land. This shows that in the earlier instance from the second phase, where *udranga* was given in one case, was now accompanyied by the right to an additional tax i.e. *Uparikara* (*CII,* Vol. IV Part I: 20, line 9). Thus, the revenue system had become more evolved than the second phase by Subandhu's time.

In social sphere, we find the culmination of the development of Brahmanical influence in Subandhu's grant. This is evident from the format of the grants themselves. While the grants of the earlier phases simply mentioned the donation aspect without mentioning any cause behind the donation, the grants of the third phase state that Subandhu had granted the village 'for acquiring merit (*Puṇya*) for his parents and for himself' (*EI*, XIX: 262-263, line 4), thus, we see an increasing influence of the Brahmanical ideals in Phase III, which prescribed donation of land as one of the means of acquiring merit. Thus, while the *Brahmadeyas* of Phase II were an attempt by the ruler to patronage a certain belief-system, in the third phase, the grants became an instrument through which the ruler expressed his affiliation with this particular belief – systems, apart from the patronage-aspect of it. Thus, while Phase II showed the rulers of Valkhā as giving space to an outside influence and trying to transform their chiefdom according to its precepts, Phase III shows the ruler as living within the folds of this belief-system – it is no longer an outside influence in Phase III but has come to stay in this region.

We see a further differentiation in the Brāhmaṇa-community in Phases III, as apart from the *gotra,* the *śākhā* (*Ibid*: lines 3-4) of the Brahmans donee is mentioned, something which is not seen in the earlier phases. Thus, we can see that Brāhma□a communitiy was not only differentiated but that certain portions of *vedas* were increasingly being practised by certain specialised groups of Brāhmaṇa, again showing the existence of full-fledged Brahmanism in the third phase.

As mentioned earlier, the coexistence of two major sects shows a religious complexity in the grants of this phase. Subandu grants a village for the repair of broken parts in the *Kalāyana-Vihāra* ('*Bhagna-sphuṭita sanskārārtham*'), to provide bed, medicines, robes, food etc to monks and for the offer of garland, *bali, sattra,* rites for the Lord Buddha (*Ibid*: lines 2-7). The mention of the grant for repair-work shows that the caves had existed for a long time before Subandhu's grant - therefore, the need for repair-works. This is the reason for our view that the caves must have been excavated sometime in the later part of the 4th century AD. From the inscription of Subandhu, we know that the caves were excavated by one Dattaṭaka ('*Dattaṭakakārita*'; *Ibid*: lines 3-4). Since no qualifications for Dattaṭaka are given, we do not know who this person was, but the absence of any royal epithets shows that he was most probably a rich merchant or some other influential person from Valkhā, who did not hold a royal or official post. However, in the absence of further information nothing much can be said about it.

The religious complexity comes about in the references given above and also the way in which the inscription ends – by quoting the conventional verses of Vyāsa - remarkable for a Buddhist inscription. The mention of the offerings of *bali*, *sattra*, garlands, incense, perfume to '*Bhagavato Buddha*' gives us a glimpse into the kind of rituals practised by the Buddhists here – clearly they had assimilated the relics of the popular ritual-system from the first phase. Once again, the meaning of the term '*bali-sattra*' changes from the second phase, where it was used in the sense of *Mahāyajñas*. Here in the third phase, they are used in the form of popular rituals, but not for the local cults, but for Buddhism. The use of these rituals in a sense helped in identifying Buddha as a deity (references to him as a '*Bhagavat*' or divine being is significant), facilitating the newly emergent Mahayanist principles in the erstwhile Hīnayāna caves, the artistic symbolism of which will be discussed in the next chapter. The use of the verses of Vyāsa again shows the heavy influence of Brahmanism.

Thus, we can say that the Buddhist caves of Bagh represented the culmination and the converging point of all the three phases of the acculturation process. This is why a religious-complexity in the grants of Buddhist caves.

The discussion in this chapter shows that the incoming influences of various streams changed the society of Valkhā considerably. The patronage of the ruler and their desire to emulate the Guptas was an instrumental factor in this acculturation process in Valkha. The acculturation involved not only a change in the socio-religious ideas, but also affected the economy and polity. Overall, there was a homogenisation effect on Valkhā which brought it closer to the mainstream society. It is not that the indigenous systems were wiped out, but that they lost the visible-space they commanded in the first phase. In each phase, we see a gradual increase in the hold of Brahmanism and later, Buddhism step by step, the latter presenting the converging point for the trends of the three phases, through the rituals and the ritual terms referred to in the Buddhist grant. We see a gradual evolving polity and economy, along with a transforming society and religious structure.

RELIGION AND ART
– SYMBOLISM AND ASSIMILATON

The acculturation process and the incoming elements in Valkhā included not only Brahmanism but also Buddhism - and from some point in the second phase onwards - they coexisted, as has been shown in the previous chapter. The inscriptions from Valkhā however, do not mention the existence of Buddhism; it was left for the last inscription available to us, from Māhiṣmatī and not from Valkhā, to give some reference to the Bagh Caves, which lie ironically, not close to Māhiṣmatī but close to Bagh or the Valkhā centre. Perhaps we should look for the cause of this in the historical process going on in this region. In the second phase, the monastery existed right next door to the Valkhā centre, but perhaps it did not play a very significant role in the socio-economic history. However in the third phase, when Valkhā was ruled from a commercially important centre like Māhiṣmatī and when the trade route from Māhiṣmatī to Bhārukaccha passed through Valkhā territory, the commercial significance of the Buddhist monastery of Bagh increased, as it lay not very far from Māhiṣmatī – Bharukaccha route. Here, it is important to note that the excavator of the caves, Dattaṭaka, may have been a trader. Moreover, Subandhu integrated the erstwhile Valkhā chiefdom in his territory and attempted to assert his control of the region through land grants to the Brāhmaṇas and the Buddhist monastery. Thus, Bagh caves become significant in this period.

Since this is the only grant giving us any information regarding the Bagh caves and Buddhism, it is necessary to use another method to obtain information about the Buddhism of the region, as we have seen that it was also a strong influence on the region, apart from Brahmanism. This method is employed through studying the art and architecture of the caves, including the architecture, sculptures and paintings, to get an idea about how the artistic symbolism were used here to express the kind of Buddhism existing here, and how the popular cults were being assimilated in the Buddhist ritual and iconography, which is the main concern of the chapter. In the following sections, we deal with how the architecture, sculptures and paintings of Bagh caves show the subtle features of the changing monastic organisation and also, how artistic symbolism was used to sustain a transforming Buddhism from *Hinayana* to *Mahayana* during the fifth century AD.

Architectural Composition

It is worthwhile to compare the architectural composition of Bagh caves with that of the contemporaneous caves of Ajanta, the nearest and the most prominent Buddhist monastic complex at the time, since it gives us an idea about how Bagh differed from Ajanta in its artistic expressions, which were found to suit the specific needs of the religion of the monastery of Bagh.

Ajanta and Bagh monastic complexes differ to a considerable degree not only in their layout, but also in the composition of the caves. While Ajanta has some caves combining the functions of *Caitya* and *Vihāra* and others where a distinct *Caitya* plan is followed, Bagh does not have a single apsidal *Caitya* cave. Most of the caves are of *Chaitya*–cum- *Vihāra* variety (i.e. shrine-cum-monastic residence) and there is only one instance of a *Vihāra* cave, with provisions for occasional gatherings.

Chronologically, cave numbers 11, 7, 6 and numbers 15 to 20 of Ajanta are contemporaneous with the Bagh caves (Kail 1975: 80-84), which came into existence some time in the beginning of 5th century AD, or even earlier. Caves 6 and 7 of Ajanta combined the residential cells with the chapel, just like the caves at Bagh. However, they show variations in their plan, while Bagh caves are more or less uniform in plan. For example, cave no. 6 of Ajanta is double-storeyed, while cave no. 7 has two small porches which lead to a verandah at the rear wall of which are cells on either side of antechamber (*Ibid*: 80-84). Such a plan is absent in Bagh. Since Bagh shows some indication of the advent of Mahayanism at some stage (as will be shown later), it is worthwhile to look at cave 19 of Ajanta which is an example of *Mahāyāna* rock-cut caves. It maintains the orthodox plan of a pure *Caitya* cave without any residential cells. A striking feature of these caves is that they are apsidal in design with pillars along the apsidal wall and the votive object based at the tapering end. However, at Bagh all the caves are either oblong or square in shape; no apsidal caves are found here. The *stūpas* too are different at Bagh and Ajanta. At Bagh the *stūpa* is a typical *Hīnayāna stūpa*, while at Ajanta, the Buddha image invariably is carved on the *stūpas* of the contemporaneous caves, showing the unty in the symbolism of Mahayanist image and the *stūpa*. At Bagh, this similarity is shown in a different manner, which will be discussed later. These differences show that the rituals of worship and the stage of Mahayanism practised in these two places were different. Also, these may show that Bagh followed a regional variation in architectural composition. As the religious aspects of Ajantan architecture and sculpture are beyond the scope of this work, we will look into the details of the form of Buddhism practised at Bagh and also, the artistic symbolism employed here.

Looking at the architectural lay-out of Bagh, it is obvious that it was a relatively well-knit monk body staying here, with its hierarchical rankings marked out (For a detailed discussion on this theme see Verma 1997: 81-94), although smaller in strength than that at Ajanta. Although it is not possible to know exactly what the strength of the monk-community of Bagh was, there are about ninety extant residential cells in the seven preserved caves of Bagh. Taking into account that nos. 8 and 9 have collapsed, the housing capacity of this *Vihāra* – complex seems to have been sizeable, although less than that of Ajanta.

Looking at the plan of Bagh caves, it appears that a major part of the monastic complex was executed at one point of time, each cave with a definite purpose and later on some additions were made as the need arose because of the growing *sangha*. There is also a possibility that some additions were made during 'repairs' referred to by Subandhu. There is some evidence of a few additions made particularly in caves 2 and 3 which will be discussed below. However, the precise date when they were added is not certain, since there is no record of it, but it could well be towards the close of the century.

The caves are designed in such a manner that each cave forms a *Caitya*-cum-*Vihāra* complex in itself (except nos. 5 and 6), serving the purposes of residence, worship and religious congregation at once, thus fulfilling the needs of the resident monks in each cave. In this sense, each cave can be called a self-sufficient monastic unit.

These characteristics can be seen in the architecture of caves 2, 4, 7 and 3. Cave 1 seems to have been excavated as an experimentation work before starting the whole excavation, as it contains only a small hall with four pillars, having no *stūpa* or cells. Caves 2, 4 and 7 follow a more or less uniform design. This includes a large pillared hall, almost square in shape, with residential cells on three sides. The wall facing the entrance has an antechamber in the middle, flanked by cells on both sides and leading on to a chamber which houses the *stūpa*. Thus, the cells housed the residual monks, the *stūpa* excavated within the cave was the votive object and the central hall provided the space for sacred gatherings, carrying out of rituals and offerings of prayers etc. This kind of plan suggests a communal form of worship offered by the residents of each cave, probably led by one or more chief monks, who perhaps resided in the cells closest to the antechamber described above.

While caves 2 and 7 follow identical plans and cave 4 is similar to the pan described above, it is to be seen that the latter is larger in size than the former and also has more number of cells - showing that the group of monks living here was larger in size. It is also significant that the cells adjacent to the *stūpa* are more in number. Moreover, this cave does not have any antechamber leading to the chapel containing the *stūpa*; one can approach the chapel directly from the hall.

Caves 3 and 5 & 6 are of special importance as they throw light on the religious aspect of Buddhism practised here as well as the hierarchical structure of the monk community of the monastery. Caves 5 & 6 are the only ones in the whole group which are connected by a small passage; other caves maintaining their aloofness from each other, to be entered from the main entrance. A look at the lay-out of cave 5 explains the peculiarity of these two caves. Cave 5 is in the form of a retangular hall, with two rows of eight pillars each in the middle, along the length of the hall and a high-rise pedestal-like projection in between the first pillars of the two rows, referred to by John Marshall as a seat (Marshall et al 1927: 15; n1). He says that this hall served either as a refectory or an oratory, as appearing from its plan (*Ibid*: 15). M. D. Khare's illustration (Khare 1971: Fig. 5) and a visit of the present writer to the caves revealed a narrow drain running all around the length and breadth of the hall, along its walls. This shows a mechanism for the draining out of water, perhaps used for washing hands before eating or offering prayers. Considering that a 'seat' is provided at the head of the row of pillars and that the drain exists, it shows that this hall was used for both ritual feasts and/or the accompanying prayers or other sacred gatherings of monks.

In this connection, it is important to note that Subandhu's grant to the caves discussed in the last chapter mentions the maintenance of alms-house/ feasts (*'sattra'*) as one of the objects to be fulfilled with the grant (*EI*, XIX: 262-263, line 5). This shows not only that the feasts to monks were a regular feature of the sacred gatherings of monks, but that this feature got a support from the ruler and it influenced the architecture of the caves to some extent. This congregational-refectorial nature of cave 5 is also highlighted by the plan of adjacent cave 6, which is connected to cave 5 by a small passage. Cave 6 is a small hall with four pillars, with cells on three sides – those on only one side are extant now. The fact that this cave is interconnected to the cave 5 - the only such interconnection found in the whole group - shows that this cave served as a place for making arrangements, preparation of meals etc. (although no hearth is found), which were carried on to the cave 5 though the passage which is quite board. Thus, there is a direct relation between the two caves. The cells around cave 6 also suggest that these were occupied by people engaged in preparation activities related to the feasts, rituals etc.; whether they were members of the monk community or lay employees of the monastery is not known. The *Mahāvagga* mentions *Bhaṇḍāgārika* i.e., overseer of stores (Bhagavat (Ed.) 1944: Verse VIII/8) and *Cullavagga* mentions *Khādyabhājaka* i.e., apportioner of food (Oldenberg (Ed.) 1880: Verse VI/4/3), showing that there was a mechanism using workers for preparation for ritual gatherings and feasts. This functional aspect of this twin cave-complex also explains the absence of a *stūpa* chamber in cave 6 – the only cave with cells which does not have a chapel. This is because the cells were used by attendants of the sacred gatherings and during *sattras,* as Subandhu's plate describes the feasts or the alms distribution ceremony.

Cave 3, although residential in nature having a stūpa, is somewhat different from caves 2, 4 & 7. It is a rectangular hall with two rows of four columns each in the middle along the length of the hall and cells on the two long sides. The third wall opens into another hall, again having two rows of columns along its length in the middle. The two halls of the cave lie perpendicular to each other, one surrounded by cells and the other without any cells. John Marshall's work says (Marshall et al 1927: 10) that the inner hall led to another court without any cells on the other side (now ruined). The whole composition of this cave shows that although it was residential, its functions exceeded simply residence and worship by the ordinary monks of Bagh caves. John Marshall mentions that going by the extra-ornateness of the cells and the walls, it must have been a cave for the superior monks of the community (*Ibid*: 10). This is evident also from the existence of two halls on both sides of the central hall – suggesting a special function for these halls – thus indicating the prominent position of the residents of cave 3 among the monk-community of this monastery. It appears that on special occasions, the resident monks, who held high ranks within the *Sangha*, performed ritual ceremonies in front of the chapel and the rest of the monk-community stood attendant in the two halls referred to earlier. Mardshall says that the outer hall is a later addition as appears from the remnant of carvings near the doorway leading to it (*Ibid*: 11). This shows that the monk community grew in time and therefore, a need arose to excavate another assembly-hall. Probably, the gathering included lay followers as well as the monks.

From the Buddhist sources, we know of some practices which had congregational aspects. For example, *'Uposatha' ceremony* comprised of the recitation of the rules of disciplines on eighth, fourtheen and fifteenth day of the fortnight. The monks were also required to attend to lay visitors on the fourteenth and fifteenth day of the fortnight (Bhagavat (Ed.): Verse 11/1/1). *'Pavāraṇa' marked* the return of the dry season and in this ceremony each *Bhikṣu* requested the assembly to point to him any incident of his having been found quilty of misconduct through speech or action during the *Vassāvāsa* or the rainy season of retreat which they had spent in the monastery (Upasaka 1975: 198) *Kaṭhina* involved distribution of robes to the monks (*Ibid*: 60). Since we have the evidence of two gathering places, one in cave 3 and another in cave 5, it is possible that both the places were used for different kinds of gatherings. This is also evident from the fact that cave 5 is provided with a seat, showing the gathering was led by a single leader, while cave 3 has no such arrangement, showing that the gathering was a common one, standing in front of the precept-residents who also stood during the ceremony (or they all sat on the floor). Thus, the leadership of the gatherings differed in both the caves. This shows that gatherings like the distribution of robes, preaching of sermon by a major monk who was either a resident or a visitor to the caves etc., apart from the *sattra* gatherings were held in cave 5, while a common recital of principles, meetings with the laity, observance of rituals concerned with the special occasions related to the *stūpa* etc., were held in the cave 3, the resident of this cave taking a leading part in these ceremonies. On normal days of course, the *stūpa* was meant for the use of the resident monks of cave 3.

From the above discussion, we can see that the architectural composition of the caves shows not only form of Buddhism practised here, but also gives us insight into the finer details of these practices. Also, we get an idea of the hierearchial set-up of the monk-community living here. As has been shown, the highest authorities lived in cave 3. Below them were some residents of cave 2, 4 and 7 and probably 8 and 9. Caves 8 and 9 have collapsed; hence no analysis can be made. The residents near the chapel were probably more important than the others and they might have led the daily worship ceremony. Below these were the vast majority of the monks who resided in the cells of the caves 2, 4, 7 and probably 8 and 9. Still lower than these were the attendance of the ceremonies, their cells in cave 6 - they may or may not have been monks, or were perhaps going through the *parivāsa* phase i.e., the phase of intervention between entering the monastery and ordnance (Upasak 1975: 144-145). At the tail end were the *upāsakas* who were only occasional visitors to the caves and did not reside there. Their existence as a possibility suggests that Buddhism appealed to the local people and attempted to carve out a support-base amongst them. The hierarchy of the monk-body shows that it was a well-developed monastery with clear functions laid out for each member. Architectural composition helps us in understanding this hierarchy.

Iconography and Religious Content

The religious aspects of the Buddhist monastery at Bagh, as discerned from the architecture can be complimented by the nature of iconography found there. They show not only the Buddhist conception about their deities, but also the influences of the popular cults on the monastic religion. The major sculpted object, and also the object of veneration in all the residential caves, as has been stated earlier, is the *stūpa*, housed in a cell and in caves 2 and 7, approached from an antechamber. The *stūpas* are mounted on a cylinder, which has an octagonal base.

Cave 2 apart from the stūpa, shows groups of Buddha images with attendants, and also, single attendants in the antechamber. These are the only Buddha-and-attendant sculptures extant now. If one looks at the records of Dr. Impey (Impey 1856 Reprinted 1969), who visited the caves sometime in 1850 and the diagrams of Maj. CE. Luard (Luard 1910) who visited the caves in 1910 and whose diagrams are based on the writings of Dr. Impey and his own visit, one will find that there was a Buddha figure on the left side verandah near the entrance of caves 2 and 4 and four figures of Buddha on the exterior wall of the area between caves 5 & 6. The figures described as found outside caves 2, 4 and 6 are barely visible now, not showing any identifiable features. However, their palcement in a monastery where *stūpa* was being worshipped throws a light on the form of Buddhism being practised here. This means that the Buddhism of Valkhā showed the point of junction between the *Hīnayāna* and

Mahāyāna, the former revering the stūpa, the latter worshiping the Buddha image.

The Buddhists sculptures at Bagh represent that stage of Buddhism, where the influence of *Mahāyāna* affected the monastery enough to introduce the Buddhists icons in the premises of the monastery, but not enough for them to replace the *stūpa* or even to superimpose or combine with it as in Ajanta, although Mahayanism was acknowledged by the community (no particular Buddhist sect is mentioned at Bagh). Thus, Buddha was acknowledged as a deity to be represented in anthromorphic form, but stūpa was retained as the symbol of worship.

Here, an observation by S. J. Tambiah is important to note. He says that both the *stūpa* and the idol of Buddha are 'reminders' of the presence of Buddha, and hence their veneration acts as a 'field of merit' in which the worshipper can harvest the religious merit. In this sense, psychologically, there is not much difference between the worshippers of *stūpa* and that of the Buddha idol, although there may be differences in their sectarian principles (Tambiah 1984: 200-204).

Taking the above into consideration, it is significant that even in an important cave like the no.3, where the high-ranking monks lived and congregational ceremonies were performed, the object of worship remained the *stūpa* – this reflects on their way of resolving the problem of identification of the object of worship. It seems that the psychological congruity in venerating the *stūpa* and the Buddhist idol as described by Tambiah must have played a significant role here – *stūpa* was perceived as signifying the same thing as did the Buddha idol, and hence, there was no necessity to replace the *stūpa* by the image even after the advent of Majayanism.

The transitional phase of Bagh monastery is also evident from the attendants shown along with the Buddha idols in cave 2. The Buddha is standing with one of his hands in *varada mudrā* (bestowing a boon), and has an *uṣnīśa (top knot)*. The left hand holds the hem of the garment in front of the shoulder. The attendant on the right of the Buddha holds a chowrie in his right hand and wears ornaments – crown and earrings, necklace, bracelets round the wrist and a thread over his left shoulder. The attendant on the left side of the Buddha has long curly locks without a crown. He too wears ornaments and holds lotus buds in this right hand. The triad on the northern wall has the same bearings. The doorway leading to the inner chapel has two single attendants. The one on the left has an elaborate *Jaṭāmukuṭa* which has a miniature Buddha seated in *Abbaya mudrā*. The attendant wears ornaments. The figure on the right is devoid of ornaments, the matted hair is tied on top with a seated Buddha in *Abbaya mudrā.* The left hand of the attendant holds a *Kamaṇḍalu* as described by John Marshall (Marshall et al 1927: 34).

Regarding the identification of these images, it is to be observed that the Buddha images of early mediaeval period onwards, are flanked by Bodhisattavas who generally represent *Maitreya* and *Padmapāṇi Avolokiteśvara* (*Ibid*: 31) the former is plainer in appearance, holds a *Nāgapuṣpa* and has a miniature *stūpa* in its crown, while the latter holds a lotus in his left hand and has *Amitābhā* in *dhyāna mudrā* in its hair (*Ibid*: 31-32; Getty 1928: 60-62).

These are the descriptions of these Bodhisattvas as they emerged from eighth century onwards. However, we have to keep it in mind that the Bagh caves are much earlier in date. Thus, the representations of Buddha attendants vary greatly. Firstly, both the attendants on the doorway has Buddha seated in *abhaya mudrā*, while the description of Bodhisattvas above requires the miniature *stūpa* in case of one and Buddha in *Dhyānī Mudrā* in case of the other. However, one attendant in one of the triads has a lotus bud, although in his right hand instead of his left and he does not have any *Dhyānī* Buddha in his diadem. On the other hand, one attendant on the doorway holds a *kamaṇḍalu.* It is to be noted that the mediaeval period Budhisattvas were beginning to have a *kamaṇḍalu* in their hand (Getty 1928: 61).

On the basis of the above, while we cannot definitely say that these attendants of Bagh caves were Bodhisattvas, as their representation does not totally tally with the description of the Bodhisattavs, we may say that these forms were precursors of the later full-fledged Bodhisattvas. Thus, the introduction of Mahayanism at Bagh also brought about and experimentation with the forms of Buddha attendants, which had not yet taken the shapes of Bodhisattvas, but also were a step ahead of being simply attendants, as is evident from their characteristics e.g., having a Buddha in *abhaya mudrā* etc. Thus, this attendant reflects a stage when the idea of Bodhisattvas flanking Buddha had emerged in the society, but had not yet taken a crystallised form, which came about only after the texts relating to Buddhist iconography laid down a set pattern for the attendants in later centuries. Thus, these attendants further show the transitory stage of Buddhism at Bagh caves.

There is also a minor figure on the exterior of cave 4 on the right side of the doorway, which suggests the experimentation stage of Bagh sculptures. This figure is supposed to be of the river deity Ganga (Khare 1971: Figure 40 A) – commonly found elsewhere in Gupta period. However, a closer look at the representation of this figure shows that this was another one of the fluid visual idioms which had not taken concrete shape yet, not at least in a peripheral region like Bagh. The female figure is standing on the '*Makara*' motif, as is the case with the Ganga sculptures. Her left hand is also on the head of a dwarf or a child, again following the set norm. However, her right hand is raised and she holds the branch of a tree which forms the canopy over her head – as against the typical river deities, who hold water pots in one hand, symbolising their association with water. Here, it may be remembered that the *toraṇas* of Sanchi *stūpa* have the figure of a female who holds the branch of a tree overhead. Thus, the Bagh figure may show a stage which has transcended the Ś*ālabhañjikā* of Sanchi, but has not yet achieved the set form of the river deities. Hence, we see in this figure a combination of the traits of both the forms.

Bagh caves have also assimilated and incorporated some figures from the popular cults and given them a place on the exterior walls of the caves – suggesting the assimilative ability of Buddhism in which these cults got a space, albeit subordinate to the Buddhist figures. Although very few of these sculptures are extent now, by following John Marshall's description, we can have an idea of the minor cults represented here. To begin with, there were two representations of Nagaraja extent till the time of Marshall, one on the northern end of cave 2 and another on the north-eastern end of cave 4; the latter carved in a shrine. The former was seated in the *Lalitāsana* pose, flanked by attendants, who were probably females and bore chowries. John Marshall saw some faint traces of the cobra-hood over the central figure (Marshall et al 1927: 38-39). While this figure was seated alone, the Nāgarāja in the shrine outside was seated along with his female companion. Her hood was gone by the time of John Marshall but the seven-headed hood of the Nāgarāja was well preserved (*Ibid*: 42). Marshall describes the presence of a seated Buddha in '*Dharma-Cakra-Pravartana*' pose over this *Nāga* panel (*Ibid*: 42-43). The position of Buddha immediately over the Nāgarāja suggests the symbolic representation of Buddha as being the main deity while the popular deity was subordinate to him.

This symbolic representation of Buddha's superiority over popular cults is also denoted by a *stūpa* carving over a figure by the side of cave 4. Marshall identified this figure as a Yakṣa, on the basis of its bearing, which is similar to the Yakṣas found at Ajanta and Ellora. Marshall describes that right above the image is carved a *stūpa* with two parasols. The representation of the parasols over the stūpa shwos that the *stūpa* is depicted not only as a symbol related to Buddhism, but as a reminder to Buddha himself. The depiction of *stūpa* over the image of Yakṣa shows an attempt at representing the superiority of Buddha over the popular cult of Yakṣa. The depiction of *stūpa* as a symbolic form of the presence of Buddha is important in this sense. Here again, we see an ideational interchange in the symbolisms of *stūpa* and the figure of Buddha which was depicted over the Nāgarāja as described earlier. Thus, the inter change of identifications between *stūpa* and the Buddha image inside the cave signified a general trend enveloping the whole monastic complex – on the exterior of the caves this artistic symbolism was used to signify the superiority of Buddhism over minor popular cults. In this sense, the symbolism in art forms was used to signify the changing ideals in the religion of Bagh caves.

From the above discussions, it becomes obvious that apart from having a clear-cut monastic order and elaborate rituals in their religious systems, Buddhism in Bagh experienced a transition of the influence of Mahayanism which transformed not only the religion but also its art. On another plane, the popular cults were getting assimilated into Buddhism, over which it showed its own superiority. That the form of worship itself has incorporated the local customs of offering garlands, flowers, *bali* etc., has been described in the previous chapter on the basis of the inscription of Subandhu. It is also to be noted that this kind of worship of an idol by making such offerings is derived from the changing characer of Buddhism under *Mahāyāna* influences and increasing ritualism. Thus, the incorporation of the local ritual system actually helped in the perpetuation of the Mahayanist influence.

Paintings

Although very few paintings are left at Bagh, by taking into account the descriptions of Dr. Impey, we can form an idea of the nature of paintings that decorated the walls of Bagh. By studying these paintings, we see that in many cases, the artistic symbolism used is much the same as that in sculpture as described in the earlier section. Moreover, they give us an insight into how the local idioms transformed the style of representation of the Buddhist figures and also, the *Jātaka* story which was probably selected to decorate the walls. The choice of a particular *Jātaka* is also in some ways related to the royal patron who made donation to the caves i.e. Subandhu.

As far as painting technique is concerned, the preparation of the surface for painting was more or less the same as that of Ajanta i.e., the *tempera* technique was employed at both the places. At Ajanta, the painting is not a true frescoe, but is done in *tempera* technique. In true frescoe, the colours are applied when the plaster is still wet. In Ajanta, the base is lime, but the colours were applied when the lime had dried. Pure white lime, probably obtained from the calcite cells, was laid on very thin and fine over layers of a mixture of straw, clay and powdered rock. The lime finish was laid out a few millimetres thick, then polished with a trowel and thus condensed. On this ivory-smooth surface were applied colours obtained from minerals like red and yellow earth, malachtite green and those made from vegetable materials like madder and indigo. Binding media was gum (Chaitanya 1976: 27-28). John Marshall describes that the technique of ground preparation was more to less the same at Bagh and Ajanta, although the first coating was not laid out carefully at Bagh. Moreover, at Bagh the coating was made of the local ferruginous earth, gravel, lime and the fibres of jute and hemp. The work, however, has been done in a slipshod manner; the coat is less tenacious than at Ajanta – seeping of water through the porous rock overhead compounding the problem (Marshall et al 1927: 16-17).

Coming to the style of painting, although the authors have tried to liken the Bagh paintings to those at Ajanta (*Ibid*: 17; Pahadia 1976: 129-130 etc.), a point seems to have been missed while comparing the paintings at the two centres. The paintings of Ajanta have used a prominent light and shade effect in order to produce a three dimensional impression, especially to highlight the facial features. At Bagh, although this effect has been used to some extent, it has been played up. Moreover, at Ajanta, the delineation of the facial features have been touched up with black outline, thus making them stand out to the view of the observer. Some marking of outline is seen in the reinforcing of body-parts at Bagh; however, except for some bodhisattva paintings (figure 3), this reinforcing of body-outline and facial features by means of a black line has not been done; only a lighter shade of ochre has been used to show the eyebrows, nose and lips, thus requiring the viewer to observe more closely for these features. Thus, there is an overall underplay of reinforcement at Bagh (from personal observation of the researcher).

Apart from the above, the general surroundings of Ajanta are given an urbane look in many Jātakas, with a liberal use of city-life motifs, heavy ornamentation of subjects etc. In contrast, Bagh paintings seem to be set in natural surroundings and have plainer backgrounds. The bodies of women and high-ranking personages are decorated with ornaments, but they are not as lavish as at Ajatna. All this shows that although the basic style of painting at Bagh and Ajanta is same, Bagh represent a variant from the Ajanta school. This differentiation may have come about in Bagh because of the local influences.

Regarding the themes of the paintings, they have not been identified with any certainty. However, some attempt has been made to see them as reflections from contemporary literature. Although John Marhsall has not identified the paintings he has made a conjecture that they do not seem to relate to any even in the life of Buddha, but related some

Jātaka or *Avadāna* story (Marshall et al 1927: 46).

Before going over to the possible identification of the paintings, it would be appropriate to describe the paintings in brief. Most of the extant paintings belong to cave 4. At the very outset, at the back of the left-side varandah where the Nāga panel described in the earlier section is carved, Dr. Impey noted rows of seated Buddha figure paintings. John Marshall also talks about the painted ornamentation of cave 3, although it is impossible to tell what these paintings were like. He however, mentions the paintings of Buddha attended by kneeling worshippers (*Ibid*: 10). C. E. Luard has also given illustrations of sitting and bending monks on cell doorways of cave 3 (Luard 1910: Plate VI, figures 1 and 2). More recently, Sandhya Pandey has given illustrations of Buddha and Bodhisattva paintings from different caves, which she has tried to identify as Buddha in preaching attitude, in *'Khasarpaṇa'* pose (discussed later in this chapter) and two Lokeśvaras and Bodhisattva (Pandey 1991: Plates 3, 11, 14, 15).

It may be suggested that on ideational plane, the execution of the painting of the Buddha and Bodhisattva etc. represents the same features as does the carving of the images of Buddha and Bodhisattva. In this sense, they have the same function of reflecting the advent of Mahayanism as do the images of Buddha and Bodhisattva. This is also highlighted by the reference by John Marshall to the worshippers knelling in front of the Buddha figures_and not in front of the *stūpa*. Thus, these paintings give us further evidence of the advent of the concept of worshipping of a personified object, although the worship of the stūpa as a reminder of the presence of Buddha is retained in the chapter. Again, John Marshall mentions that the figures of kneeling worshippers in front of the Buddha are painted on the outer wall of the shrine housing the *stūpa* which is eroded now, in cave 3 (Marshall et al 1927: 10). Here again, we get evidence of the use of artistic symbolism to eatablish the identities of *stūpa* and the Buddha figure as one. Thus, the depiction of Buddha on the outer wall of the shrine symbolically states that the image and *stūpa* signify the same thing i.e., the presence of the Buddha. In this sense, painting serves the same function of signifying the artistic symbolism, as do the sculptures and carvings at Bagh – the symbolism has been extended from sculpture to painting.

The paintings of monks on the cell doorways show that cave 3 was residential. One of the monks is bare-headed, while another is wearing a head-gear, showing that this monk is of a higher rank. This is important in light of the discussion in the previous section about cave 3 as occupied by the high-ranking monks.

Regarding the identification of the Buddhist figure as *Khasarpaṇa* by Sandhya Pandey, it is worthwhile to look at the description of *Khasarpaṇa* in Buddhist iconigraphy. He is described as having the peculiar feature of being invariably_accompanied by the four divinities – Tara, Sudhana Kumāra, Bhṛkuṭi and Hayagrīva. The principal figure is two armed and one-faced. He is of white complexion and sits either in *Lalitāsana* or in *Ardhaparyanka* (Bhattacharya 1924: 37).

The Bagh figures identified by Sandhya Pandey as *Khasarpaṇa* is sitting on a lotus, one leg folded and another raised, his right hand in *Varada Mudrā* and has a halo. There seems to be a back-rest-like object provided behind him. He has a kneeling devotee in front of him with a lamp in his hand which is not lighted. The appearance hardly tallies with the description of *Khasarpaṇa* as descried in the Buddhist text, the deity in any case being of later origin than the date of Bagh caves. Thus, in all probability this is a figure of Buddha, although his pose is unsual. However, the Uṣṇīśa, elongated ear-lobes and the devotee etc. confirm that he must be Buddha. As regards Padmapāṇi etc., although their appearance also does not follow the description, their possibility of being precursors to the later Bodhisattvas has been discussed earlier in the section on sculpture.

A distinction between the Bodhisattva figures of Ajanta and those of Bagh as appears from the illustrations from Sandhya Pandey is in their ornamentation. A particular comparison can be made between The Padmapāṇis of Ajanta and Bagh (Pandey 1991: Plate 3). Both the Buddhist figures are in *Tribhanga* pose, although bending in opposite directions. The Bagh figure holds the stalk of a flower in its right hand, the flower is eroded, but by the shape of the vacant space as evident in Mukul Dey's reproduction (Dey 1925: 171, Plate LII). It appears that it was a lotus suggesting the identification of the figure as Padmapāṇi. When compared with the famous Padmapāṇi of Ajanta Cave 1 (Figure 1), it is seen that apart from the similarity in pose, expression and the characteristic of holding a louts, the conception of the Padmapāṇi by the artists at two places is very different. For, the Ajanta figure is lavishly decorated and has a luxurious appearance – his ornaments are made of expensive jewels and pearls, his crown of gold studded with gems. On the other hand, the figure of Bagh is decorated with Nature itself. His crown is only a band of metal, the rest of the head decoration done with flowers and leaves. Creepers, leaves and flowers have been used to decorate his person as well, to the extent that the Brahmanical chord over the left shoulder of the Ajanta figure has given way to the entwined double-creepers at Bagh.

This seems to be an example of the local motifs influencing the perception of the Bagh artists. The artists at Bagh has taken the local motifs and produced, with natural ornamentation of the Bodhisattva figure, an effort which is in marked contrast to the urbane and luxurious effect produced by the artist at Ajanta. This shows how the surviving elements of local culture influenced the imagination of the artist who had to follow certain set norms while depicting a deity, and could bring about a change in the conception of the divinity of the figure. This is also a case of the local elements, which were subordinated by the Brahnanical influence, got a space in the Buddhist art.

The influence of the local culture brings about a change in the concept of divinity itself. At one place, urbane luxury is considered to be a part of the pre-ascetic divinity, while at another, natural beauty takes the place of the urbane luxury and produce quite a different type of Padmapāṇi. To a somewhat lesser degree, this kind of ornamentation by natural objects is shown in two other Bagh figures of Buddha or Bodhisattva (Pandey 1991: Plate 15) (their identification not being clear), showing that this influence of the local or folk elements was not incidental. Thus, we can say that Bagh shows a variation from Ajanta in its conception of pre-ascetic Buddhist divinities as it has employed a different idiom to express their divinity.

The painted panels in cave 4 are the major works of paintings at Bagh. As has been said earlier, several attempts have been made to identify these paintings, but no definite conclusion has been reached. As most of the paintings were in a bad state even during John Marshall and Mukul Dey's times, we have to go by Dr. Impey's accounts, taking help from john Marshall's illustrations of whatever paintings were left by his time. Dr. Impey describes the long continuous panel divided into sections in cave 4, which includes a weeping woman and her royal-looking friend consoling her (figure 5), three princely figures talking to a monk-like figure wearing jewels around his neck (figure 6), five ascetics talking to an ascetic (figure 11), two groups of dancing women around two foreign-looking figures (figure 7) and a long cavalcade of horse and elephant riders (figures 9 and 10) including either higher officials or royal personages, as is evident from the parasols over them and some women riding on elephants being a part of the cavalcade. The illustrations of all these paintings are provided by John Marshall. However, Dr. Impey's account tells us that beyond this cavalcade, there were more paintings which had vanished by John Marshall's times. These paintings, as described by Dr. Impey, will be discussed later.

Krishna Chaitanya has tried to identify the royal cavalcade described above as the pleasure ride arranged by Śuddhodhana for Siddhārtha, from which the prince withdrew in the evening. He also says that the weeping woman must be Yaśodharā and the royal lady consoling her is Queen Foster Mother Gotamī (Chaitanya 1976: 43). However, it is to be noted that the whole panel described above, from the weeping woman to the royal cavalcade, relates to one event, as sections are related to each other and seen to point towards the section where three royal personages are talking to one ascetic-like person who has jewels around his neck (figure 6). Dr. Impey also remarks that it is a continuous panel. Hence, if we take the weeping woman to be Yaśodharā and the cavalcade as the pleasure ride arranged by Śuddhodhana, then the meaning of the panel is not clear, since the cavalcade does not have a painting of Siddhārtha riding in a chariot as the legend describes. Nor would the meaning of the group engaged in conversation is clear, unless we identify the ascetic-like figure as Buddha himself, which is not likely, judging from his appearance. He does not have any characteristic traits of Buddha and the jewels around his neck do not tally with Buddha's renunciation account, in which he gave away all the jewels and robes etc. to his charioteer. Krishna Chaitanya too is silent on the matter of identification of this figure.

Moti Chandra believes that the panel at Bagh does not appear to be Buddhist, but seems to be related to contemporary life. He says that the themes are nothing but the vignettes from the gosthikas as reflected in the *Caturbhāṇī*, the four burlesques of the Gupta period (Chandra 1970). The *Caturbhāṇīs* depict goṣṭhikās, in which the urbane elites or the nāgarikas took part, alongwith courtesans, attendants and friends etc. These were pleasure sessions which were held in a garden or in a grove.

Moti Chandra has perhaps based his identification on the dance scenes and the royal cavalcade described earlier. However, the scene of three royal figures conversing with a monk-like figure certainly has Buddhist content, contrary to Moti Chandra's view. Moreover, the weeping woman does not fit into his identification of the panel as the representation of a goṣṭhikā.

The above discussions shows that whatever little attempt has been made to identify the paintings of Bagh, is based on only a part of the whole panel-no author has visualised the whole panel as one single continuous account of an event, its sections having relation to each other. If we visualise the whole panel in this manner, we get certain ides about the event depicted. The happenings in the panel which emerge from observations are (1) a prince's renunciation and becoming an ascetic, but he has not attained complete monkhood yet – as seen from the necklace around his neck, (2) a royal lady, related to the prince probably, grieving over his decision to renounce the word, (3) one person of royal bearing along with two other major personalities coming to talk to the prince, (4) another ascetic, of a different nature from the ascetic-prince described above, along with five other ascetics having some relation with the whole event, (5) a royal pageant, comprising of dancing women and men, musicians, royal figures, high officials and other people, coming towards the prince – perhaps they formed the retinue of the royal figures who are conversing with the prince.

This kind of sequence of events is very familiar in the Buddhist literature as the *Jātakas* and the life-legend of Buddha talk about many royal personages becoming followers of Buddha. The reason why the renouncer-prince is not identified with Buddha himself is that he does not carry attributes of Buddha and no event in the *Buddha Carita* corresponds exactly with the sequence of events depicted here. Thus, John Marshall may be right that the panel depicts some *Jātaka* story. There is at least one *Jātaka* which relates the renunciation of a prince and seems to conform to the Bagh paintings, which is known as the *Mahājanaka Jātaka*. It has been depicted at Ajanta too, but the events depicted there are different in their form of representation from Bagh. If we look at some of the events described in this Jātaka, we find that there is some similarity in the narration and in the Bagh paintings.

The *Mahājanaka Jātaka* is a long narrative, but we are concerned here only with the latter part of the *Jātaka*, as it is this part which has been probably depicted here in part. In short, Mahājanaka decided to renounce the world. When he left the palace, his queen Śivālī sent seven hundred concubines to snare him with their charms. Mahājanaka was unperturbed and carried his journey onwards to the Himalayas. The queen was greatly grieved and went after Mahājanaka, followed by all the army, people and the animals for riding. A sage called Nārada, who had just attained the perfect bliss, decided to encourage the king to pursue his path inspite of the dissuasion of these people. Nārada came flying in the air, talked to Mahājanaka and left, flying in the air again. Nārada is said to have attained five supernatural powers, which are not named (Cowell: Vol VI, 30; 31-33). This is the portion of the *Jātaka* which is of interest to us. The story goes on to relate the renouncer – prince's onward journey and the queen and the other people's repeated entreaties to him to turn back, and his efforts to prove to the queen that he no longer belongs to the world. However, this later part is of no concern to us, as the paintings at Bagh show similarities with the portion of the story narrated above.

The reference to seven hundred concubines who were sent by queen Śivālī to ensnare Mahājanaka may be represented by the two groups of the dancing women, along with the women musicians (figure 7). Again, the grieving Śivālī may be represented by the weeping woman, who is being consoled by her royal friend (figure 5). The group engaged in discussion with the monk-like figure shows the efforts of the royal family members and the royal officials to try to persuade Mahājanaka, while the royal cavalcade fits the description of the queen being followed by "all the army, people and the animals for riding" (Ibid: 31-32), when she went after Mahājanaka. The mention of Nārada's visit to Mahājanaka by the aerial path may be seen in the ascetic-like figure surrounded by five more figures like himself (figure 11). It is to be noted that the ascetic surrounded by five figures, has been described by John Marshall as "flying and issuing forth from the clouds" (Marshall et al 1927: 48). It is also noteworthy that Nārada has five supernatural powers (Cowell: 32) and the ascetic described above is surrounded by five figures. The supernatural faculties, evil and good tendencies etc. are often depicted in human form in Buddhist art. The depiction of Temptation *Māra* in personified form is well known. Thus, it is possible that the supernatural powers of Nārada were painted as anthropomorphic forms surrounding him.

We can see that there are certainly some similarities in the motifs of narration and the motifs of depiction. Hence, it may be suggested that the panel at Bagh possibly represents a portion of the *Mahājanaka Jātaka*. There are, however, also some variations. For example, the *Jātaka* describes the king going away and the queen, the officials and the crowd following him. On the other hand, this painting gives the impression of the renouncer-prince sitting in a grove while the queen grieves and the stately figures of the court try to dissuade him. It is also noteworthy that while Ajanta starts from an earlier point in the story in Cave 1 when Mahājanaka was ruling as a king, and later he decided to stay at the top of the palace as a sage and finally, the queen and the royal procession alongwith the masses are shown as going out of the city-gate, Bagh has captured one moment of the story, focussing on the grief of the queen and the royal officials and the people coming out of the city gate. Thus, the treatment of the same theme is different at Ajanta and Bagh. The focus on the queen's grief at Bagh again shows that folk elements of Valkhā which gave a visible-space to women, also moulded the art of Bagh caves.

Here, a slight discussion on the forms of narrative employed in the ancient Indian mural-art would be helpful to understand the style of composition employed at Ajanta and Bagh. There are basically three kinds of narratives relevant to our study – *Synopstic narrative* takes one single event of a story and depicts it is a single picture–frame. *Episodic narrative* employs the strategy of showing the sequence in an episode, but the geographical locale does not change. *Continuous narrative* shows the movement of the story from one event to another, through a number of picture–frames (Dehejia 1997). Sometimes, two or more of these narratives modes are combined in the representation of a particular *Jātaka*. At other times, the pure forms of narrative are used. Thus, at Ajanta, the story moves through several sequences of events, hence it follows the continuous narrative form while depicting *Mahājanaka Jātaka*. On the other hand, at Bagh one captivating moment of the story has become important. However, several sections, on a long panel have been employed to depict this moment. Also, the topography remains more or less the same throughout the panel. Thus, while Synoptic narrative is the basic technique used, it combines the features of continuous as well as episodic narratives in the depiction of the *Jātaka*.

The paintings follow a realistic style of depiction instead of too much stylisation except in the case of hand-gestures etc. This again suggests the influences of the local culture on the style of painting at Bagh. This is also seen from the appearances of the figures depicted here (See Appendix II). In this sense, the style of depiction of the figures from the long panel is analagous to the departure from norms in the adornment of Bodhisattvas as describe earlier. One is struck by the relatively plainer appearance of even the royal personages, as against the figures of Ajanta, which are normally bedecked with Jewels. Perhaps this style at Bagh represents a different idiom of depiction from Ajanta, and the difference created by the local folk elements, subordinated by the Brahmanism, which were getting a space in Buddhism.

As in sculpture, in painting too, we see the artistic symbolism used, some of which has already been described before. This is again seen in Dr. Impey's account of a painting which is lost now. It tells us that beyond the cavalcade described above, there were more paintings which had vanished by John Marshall's times. He notes that "this panel consists of four elephant and three horses, which seem to have arrived at their destination and are at rest, and so are the mohouts. Their gaze is fixed on a mango tree, under which are two small frames containing drinking vessels and a gourd. Close to these a piece of cloth with blue ends is suspended from a branch and beside it is a *cakra*. Further on, under a plantation tree is a figure of Buddha (although it is an unusual description), seated cross–legged and clothed, holding his right hand in his left and beside him a discipline listening to the doctrine he is expounding. He differs from Buddhist figures in general in being without curly hair and therefore, resembles other figures" (Impey 1856 Reprinted 1969: 564).

If the Buddha figure described by him is really Buddha, then it depicts the event of *Dharma-Cakra –Pravaratana*, for his description of the figure's right hand held in the left one is a typical *Dharma-Cakra Pravartana* gesture. But Dr. Impey's statement that the Buddha is without his curly hair suggests that he could be either the Buddha or another monk preaching preaching to a disciple. The presence of the wheel however, is typical of the *Dharma-Cakra Pravartana* depiction. On the other hand, the wheel may symbolise the presence of the Buddha while the monk is preaching to the discipline - thus empowering the preacher. The symbolism of *cakra* here is again important in that not only it denotes the presence of the Buddha but also empowers the preacher. However, since the painting has long ago vanished, nothing much can be said about it. The paintings of Bagh caves thus, show similarities with sculpture in using artistic symbolism to signify the presence of the Buddha.

The discussions in this chapter give us insights into not only the religious aspect of Buddhism, but also into how the artistic expressions were used to signify the finer details of this outside influence which coincided with the Brahmanism discussed in the previous chapter, both in space and in time. Apart from the direct information about Buddhism e.g., hierarchy in the monk-body and the advent of Mahayanism at Bagh, the art – expressions tell us how artistic symbolism was used to signify various features which had become integrated into the Buddhism of Bagh. Assimilation of popular cults, influence of local culture, use of painting to denote power and the conception of a personified deity (i.e. Buddha), psychological congruity between the meanings of stūpa and image, use of a *Jātaka* to signify the concept of renouncer-prince who resembles the Buddha in life-narrative etc., are some of the finer aspects which emerge from the study of the works of art of the caves. An important feature which comes out of this study and is not known from the inscriptions is the revelation that the elements of local culture, which were overshadowed by the acculturating influence of Brahmanism, not only received a space in Buddhism, but also influenced its arts and ritual.

This complex interplay of various streams in the visual art of the caves arose because of the transformation of Valkhan society described in the previous chapter. Buddhsim in *Hīnayāna* form was increasingly sidelined with the advent of Brahmanism in Valkhā. However, once an agrarian base came to be established In Narmada region with the help of Brahmanical ideology, Valkhā's revival as a Buddhist centre would certainly have required change in Buddhism of a kind similar to the Brahmanical forms of worship and ritual which only Mahayanism could provide. Hence, Subandhu's renovation of the Bagh caves could well be associated with the introduction of Mahayanist forms and ideals.

It is possible that there is political allegory behind the choice of a *Jātaka* dealing with the life of renouncer prince as the disappearance of the territory of Valkhā from the historical visibility after Subandhu tempts one to ask whether Subbandhu did not pursue exercise of power. However, in absence of more conclusive evidence regarding this possibility, it can only be posed as a question.

OVERVIEW

The foregoing discussion in this work shows that the visual art of Valkhā represents the religious assimilation by Buddhism, an approach caused by the processes of transformation that took place through three successive phases, as shown by the analysis of the inscriptions. As a result of this transformation, we find that Valkhā saw the emergence of a dominant class composed of various categories of Brāhmaṇas. However, this being an early state of transformation of Valkhan society, we do not find certain features of Brahmanisation here which are evident in some other regions e.g., there is no use of a genealogy by the ruling chief of Valkhā. These ruling chiefs apparently did not belong to a single descent group or lineage as no attempt is made in the inscriptions to mention the relationship of one chief to another, although all of them, in some way or the other, show a subordinate relationship with the Gupta rulers. Besides, there isn't evident a well-developed *Varṇa* – structure. We only come across various categories of Brāhmaṇas and the mention of some professional groups e.g., potter, the trading group suggested in the name 'Vaṇijaka' etc. Thus, the acculturation process in Valkhā shows the establishment of a strong Brahmanical idiom as evident from the inscriptions, but not with all its features.

An impact of the emergence of Brahmanical ideal in Valkhā was coincident with a simultaneous overshadowing of certain local or popular ideals or their incorporations into the Brahmanical stream in such a manner that they were given a complete Brahmanical appearance. The transformation of the *'bali-cāru-sattra'* offerings used by the local cults into the Brahmanical *Mahāyajñas* of *'bali-sattra-vaiśvadeva* as discussed in the chapter on religious transformation reflects the tendency of the emergent Brahmanism to give the popular rights a Brahmanical garb. On the other hand, it has been discussed earlier that women got a visible-space in the first phase of land-grants when the local idiom was still strong in Valkhā but from the second phase onwards, women become almost invisible in the inscriptions. This reflects a case of the Brahmanical norms overshadowing the pre-existing popular norm which gave a prominent space to women.

More or less the same tendency is evident in the fact that the patronage to the female deities i.e., the Bhagavatīs in the first phase, vanishes with the emergence of the dominant Brahmanism – suggesting an overshadowing effect. Thus, we can see that the Valkhā of 4th-5th centuries of the Christian era had started showing the emergence of the traits of the Puranic religion which went hand-in-hand with the Brahmanical dominance in the later centuries. The Brahmanical influence was so strong in Valkhā by the last phase studied here, that even the Buddhist grant was inscribed in a Brahmanical idiom – as discussed in an earlier chapter.

With the emergence and strengthening of the Brahmanical ideal, the pre-existing Buddhism in Valkhā could reinvigorate itself only by transforming itself in such a way that it both resembled the Brahmanical form of ritual and worship and appealed to the popular levels by giving space to some of the idioms from the popular culture. We come across the evidence from this in epigraphs as well as the visual sources from Bagh. The mention of the *'mālya-bali-sattra* with reference to *Bhagavato-Buddhāya* in the Buddhist grant reflects the efforts of the monastic sect to transform its worship and ritual to resemble the Brahamical rituals described earlier. Also, as this ritual system was already known to the popular cults in Valkhā, it made a distinct appeal at the popular level.

Another transformation in the Buddhism of Bagh consequent upon the strengthening of Brahmanism here is the transformation of the erstwhile Hīnayānism to Mahāyānism by 'repairs' carried out by Subandhu as discussed in the chapter on art-symbolism, which also indicate a possible embellishment of the of the caves.

Buddhism's attempt to appeal to the popular level is also evident from its visual art, which attempted the assimilation of local or folk forms in its religion as discussed earlier. Moreover, its paintings executed in the local idiom and the *Mahājanaka Jātaka* panel focussing on the queen's misery rather than on Mahājanaka's attainment points to an attempt by the monastic art to give a visible-space to the local norms.

Thus, Brahmanism not only transformed the society and the religion of Valkhā but was also instrumental in transforming the monastic religion of Buddhism, which was consequently manifested in its visual art. In this sense, the focus on Valkhā and the Bagh caves in this work is important, as it brings into sharp focus the nature of assimilation through visual representations, especially when Juxtaposed with the contents of epigraphs. The visual art thus, reflects the flux going on between the three layers at Valkhā – the popular, the Brahmanical and the Buddhist.

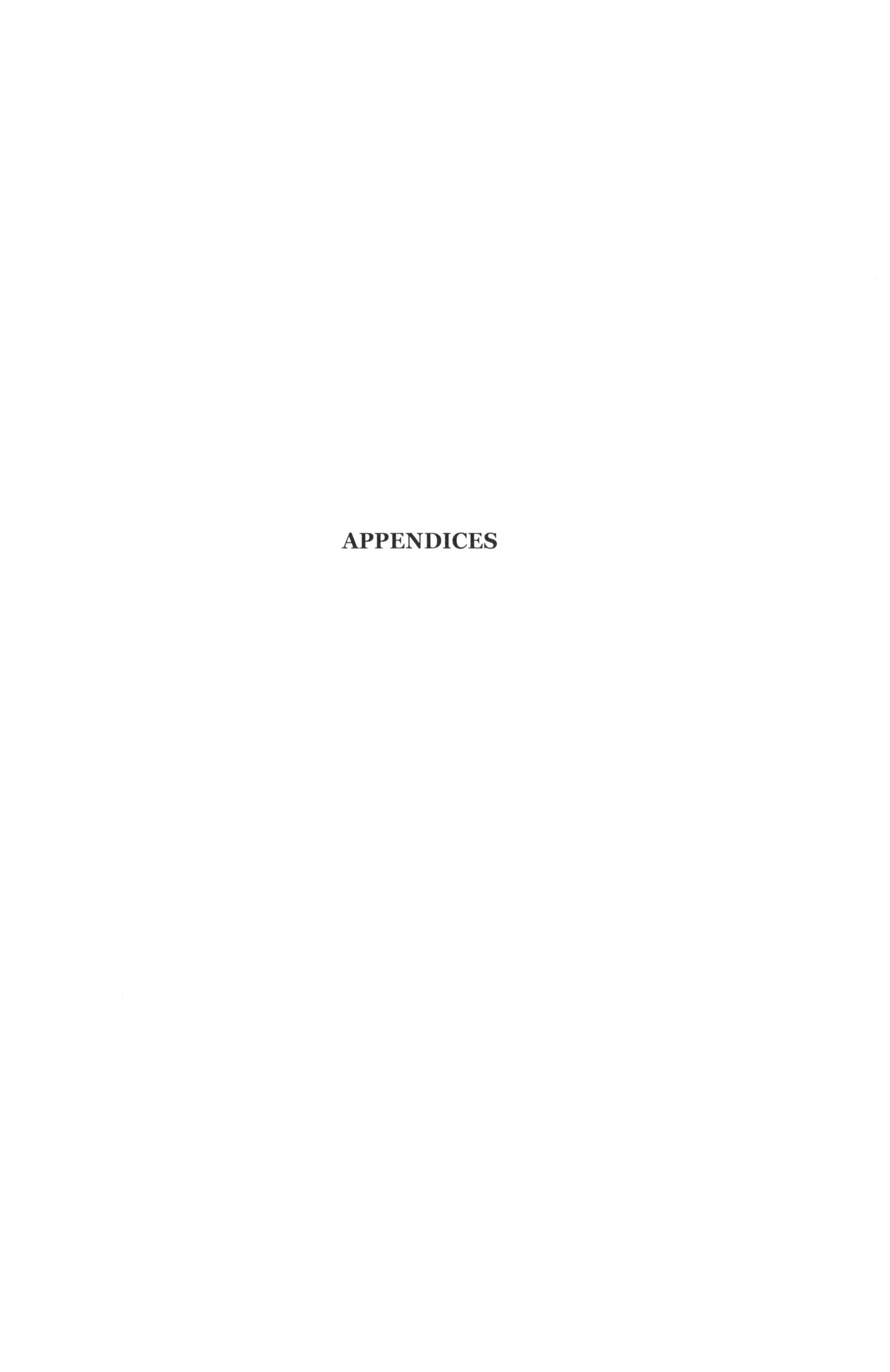

APPENDICES

APPENDIX I
Techniques of Mural Paintings at Ajanta and Bagh

In order to form an idea about the technique of painting used at Bagh and to compare it with that at Ajanta, it would be worthwhile to look at the textual injunctions in the *Viśṇudharmottaram* regarding the techniques of art-forms and therefore, closest in date to Bagh among all such texts.

Apart from the delineation and painting of forms etc., the 40th chapter of the third section of *Viśṇudharmottaram* called the *cittrasūtra*, gives a detailed account of how the ground for the mural paintings should be prepared. It says that brick-powder (*Iṣṭakacūrṇa*) of three varieties (smooth, medium and coarse) should be mixed with clay; one-third of it in proportion. To this is added fragrant gum-resin, beeswax, honey, *Kundara* grass, molasses, safflower soaked in oil, all in equal proportion ("*Guggulam Samādhūt-śiṣṭam-madhu-kundarakam/ kusumbhasma-tailsamyuktam-kṛtvā*"; Sivaramamurti 1978: 150, verses III/40/1-3). To these two parts already composed is added powder of lime (*Ibid*: III/40/2), ¾ parts burnt with *bel* – fruit pulp and lampblack. (*Ibid*: III/40/1-2). It is soaked in water stored in a pot so as to get lubricious (*Ibid*: III/40/4) and is kept so for a month. When it becomes a very soft paste, it has to be carefully taken out and a coat applied by a skilled artist on the wall after testing that it is quite dry (*Ibid:* III/40/5). The coating should be smooth, even, firm, free from uneven patches, neither too thin nor too thin (*Ibid:* III/40/6). The coating should be smooth, it should be smothered by an application of the clay bereft of *sarjarasa* and oil by coats of lime and frequent melting of the surface with milk and rubbing all with a great effort (*Ibid:* III/40/7-8). ... When the wall is dry... the artist should draw and fix-up the proportions and positions of the figures. Then he should fill figures with colours (*Ibid:* III/40/14-15). The materials for colours are gold, silver, copper, mica, lapis lazuli, red lead, yellow ochre, terraverte, lime, red lac, vermillion, indigo and many such colours (*Ibid:* III/40/25-26). For a desirable binding medium in the colours, the exudations of *Vakula* and *Sindūra* trees would be appropriate (*Ibid:* III/40/29).

The above accounts from the *Viṣṇudharmottaram* shows that the technique of preparing the ground for painting involved two layers of plastering what S. Paramasivan called coarse and fine plasterings (Bhattacharya 1979: 39). Over the fine plastering, the figures were executed and filled with colours.

The description however, is a textual one, reflecting the ideal mode of executing mural paintings, achieved by centuries of experimentations. The extant mural paintings however, may or may not have followed these guidelines exactly depending on the material available, familiarity of the artists with the texts etc. Hence it is necessary to juxtapose this description with the actual findings from the chemical analysis of the paintings of Ajanta and Bagh. These two centres have followed broadly the same technique and in general conformed to the textual description, but they also show some variations from each other and also from the texts, owing to the local availability of materials.

The scientific investigation show that in the rough plastering, mud mixed with straw husk, vegetable seeds, vegetable fibres and paddy husks were at Ajanta. The rough plaster was more of less same at Bagh, except the presence of paddy husks which was peculiar to Ajanta (*Ibid:* 38). Apart from these materials, the presence of sand also has been noted in various proportions at both the places (Bhattacharya 1979: 38). In the layer of fine plastering, both Ajanta and Bagh reveal lime as the basic material along with the small portion of gypsum (*Ibid*: 39). Thus, fibruous material is enjoined to use clay bereft of *sarjarasa* grass. However, whether oil was used as described in the text is not clear.

As for the colours used at Ajanta, Paramasivan has identified the folloing pigments – yellow ochre, red ochre, carbon, lime, terraverte, and lapis luzuli from cave 2 and terraverte and yellow ochre from cave 16 (*Ibid:* 69). A. K. Haldar's study of the pigments of the Bagh caves shows that the earthen and stone pigments used at Bagh were identical to Anjata. Apart from these, lac-dye for red was also used at Bagh (Haldar 1921: Vol. VIII, 15). Thus, we see that almsot all the colours used at Bagh and Ajanta have been referred to in the text mentioned above. However, besides these the text also mentions the use of pigments made of expensive metals which are not found at Bagh and Ajanta. Two reasons seem to be implied here – the cost of preparing the pigments as has been suggested by A. K. Bhattacharya (Bhattacharya 1979: 79) and secondly, the text shows a perfected technique reached at by experimentations of centuries, while the extant paintings show an advanced stage in this technical evolution – the use of metallic colours probably came later than this period. The use of lac-dye at Bagh shows the artist's tendency to improvise with the locally available material.

Although it is very difficult to identify the binding medium through chemical analysis, Paramasivan's analysis shows that Ajanta artists used animal extracts i.e., glue for binding the colours, while Bagh artists used the tree extracts i.e., gum for binding the colours (Bhattacharya 1979: 69, note 14) - the latter in line with the text while the former showing a tendency to experiment. It appears that after such experiments were done with pigments, binding medium etc., the texts prescribed a certain substance as 'appropriate' for use by the artists. Thus, after the experiments of Bagh and Ajanta the texts gave the injunction that the tree extract was appropriate as has been described earlier. However, it could also be the case that while the text presented an 'ideal' technique of paining, different art-centres used their own variations on the broad guidelines and therefore, there is some deviation from the texts. In any case, it appears that the textual injunction was only to be used as a guideline; it was not meant to be and was never, followed word-to-word, as only the broad instructions of the text were taken.

APPENDIX II
Visual Depictions of the Bodhisattvas and the Mahajanaka Jataka at Ajanta Cave 1 and Bagh Cave 4 – A Comparative Display

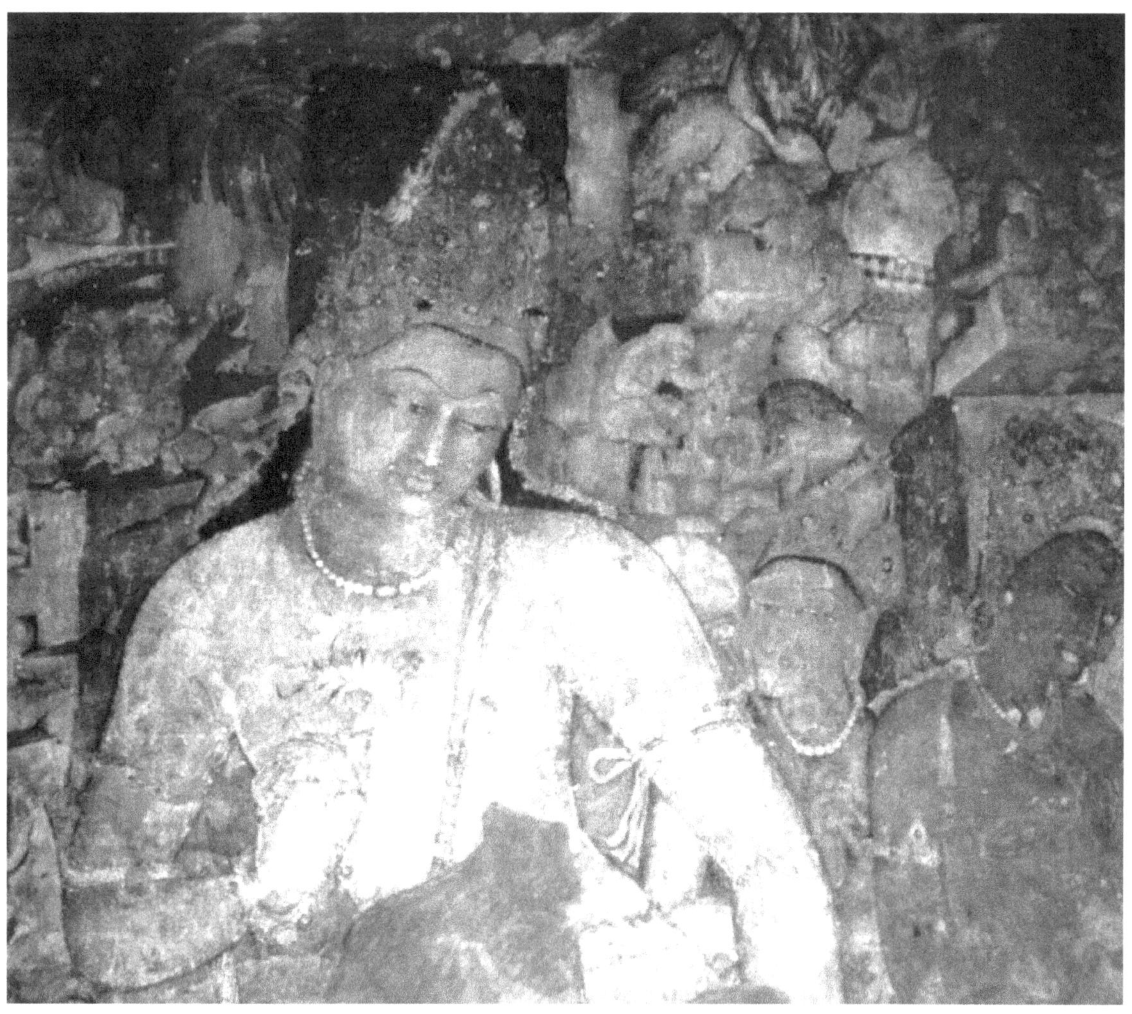

Figure 1 Ajanta Cave 1 Padmapani Bodhisattva

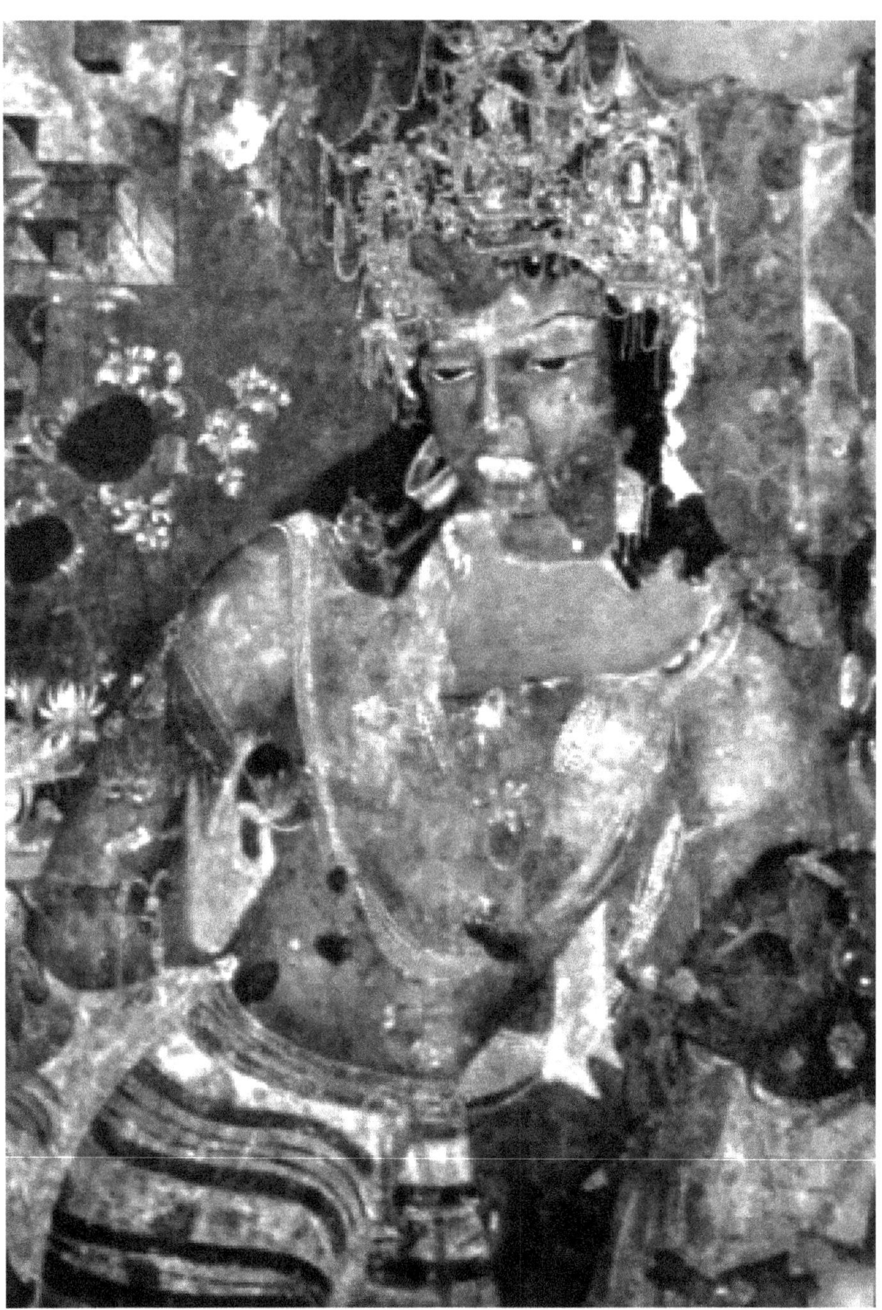

Figure 2 Ajanta Cave 1 Vajrapani Bodhisattva

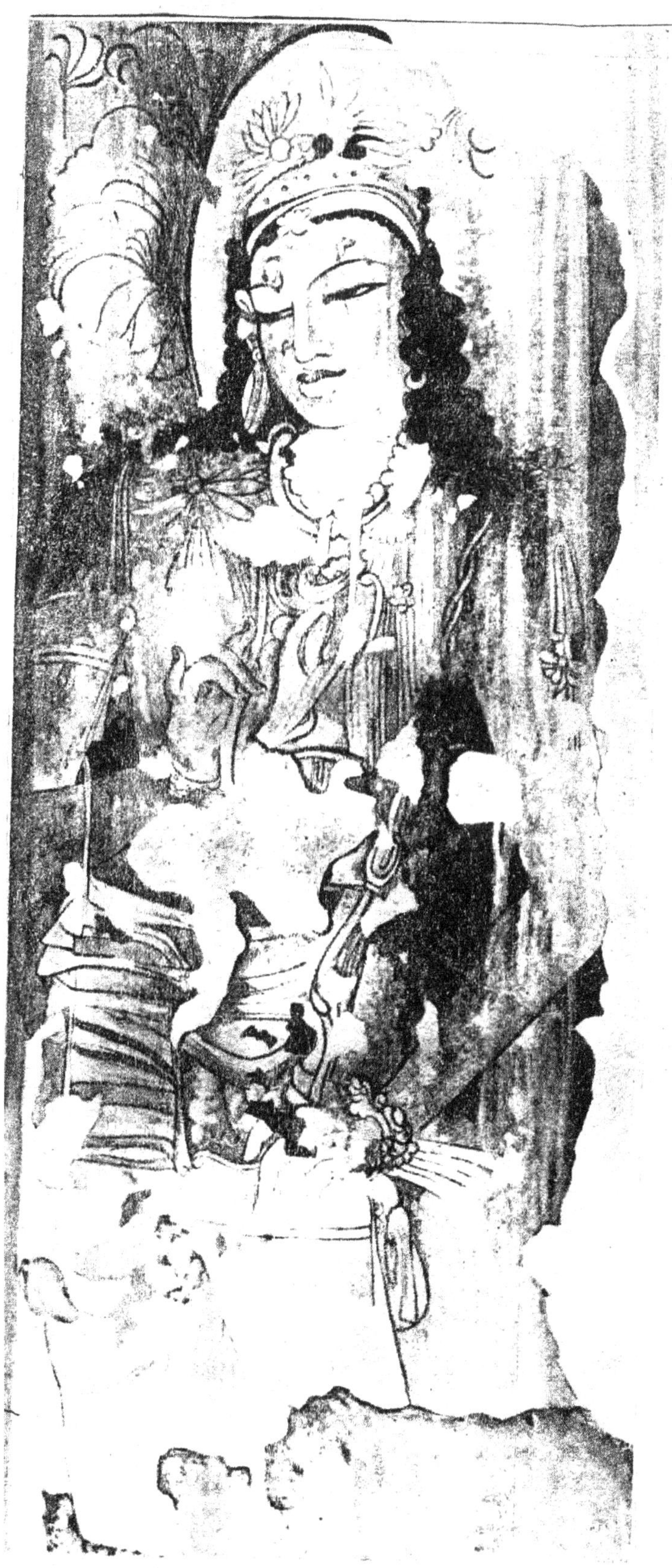

Figure 3 Bagh Cave 2 Padmapani Bodhisattva

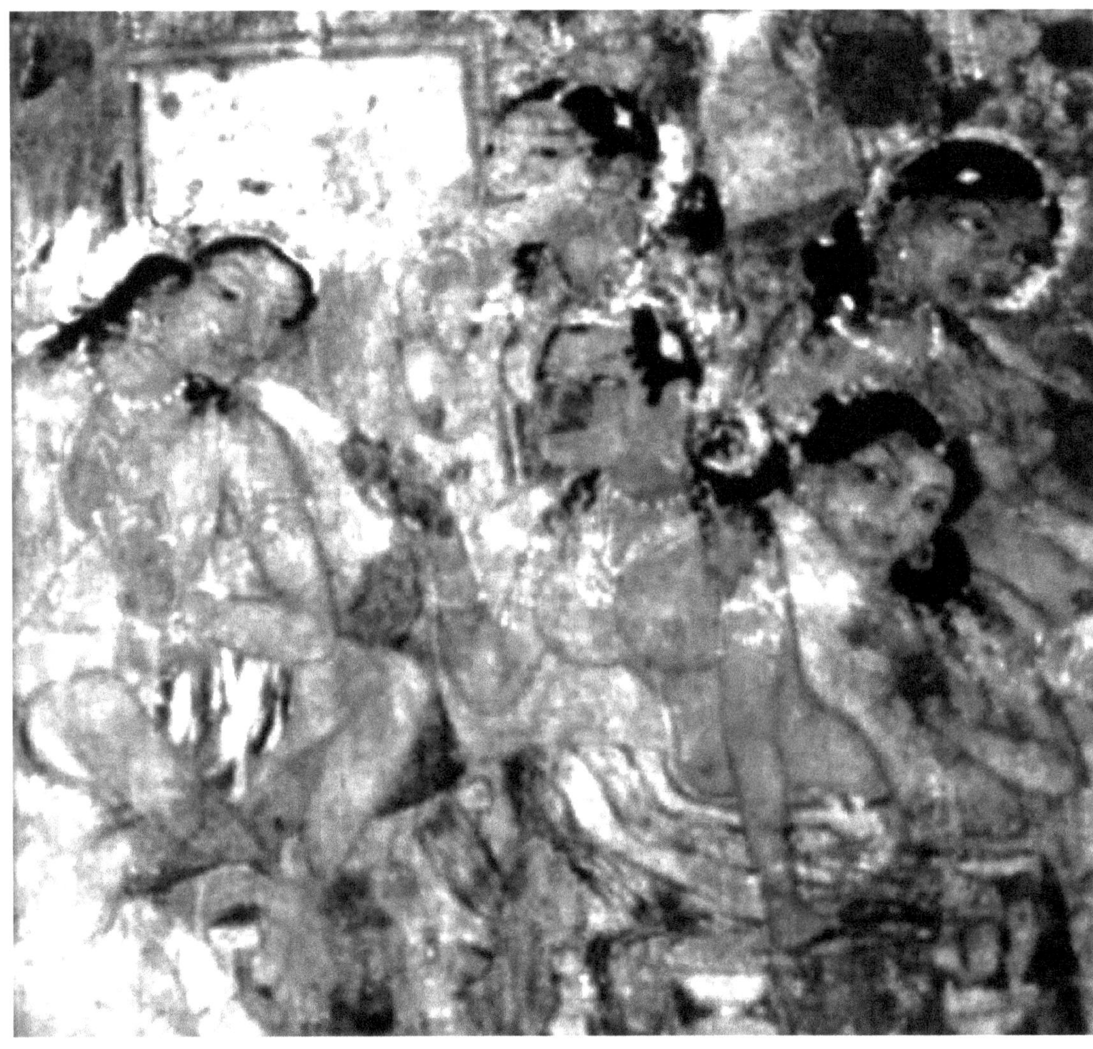

Figure 4 Ajanta Cave 1 Anxiety of Shivali and the Palace Women at Mahajanaka's Decision to Renounce the World

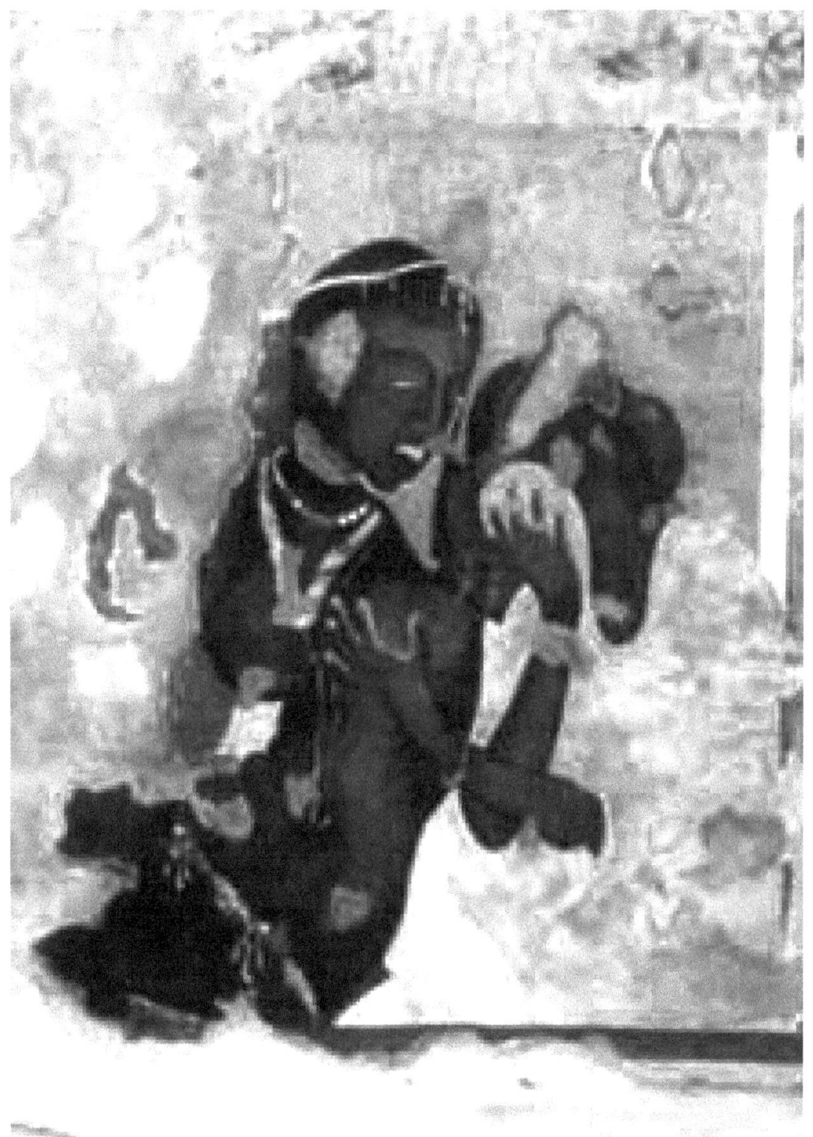

Figure 5 Bagh Cave 4 Grieving Shivali at Mahajanaka's Decision to Renounce the World

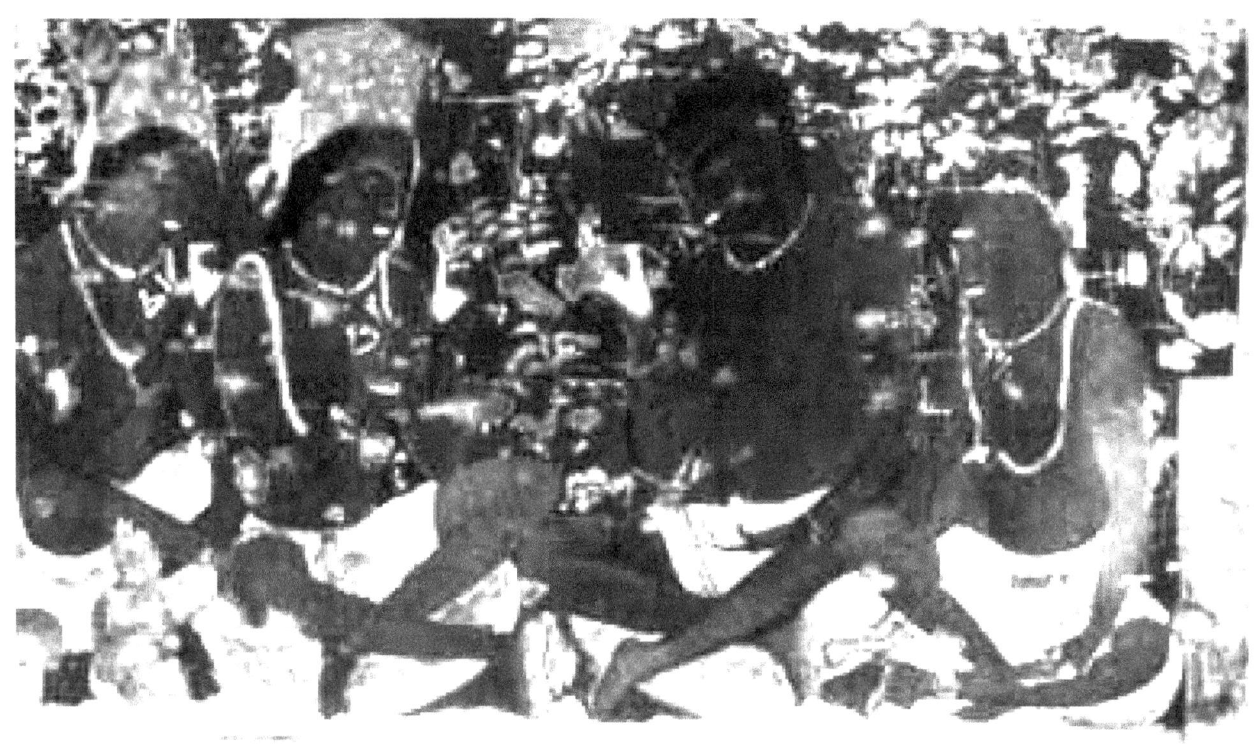

Figure 6 Bagh Cave 4 Mahajanaka's Decision to Renounce the World

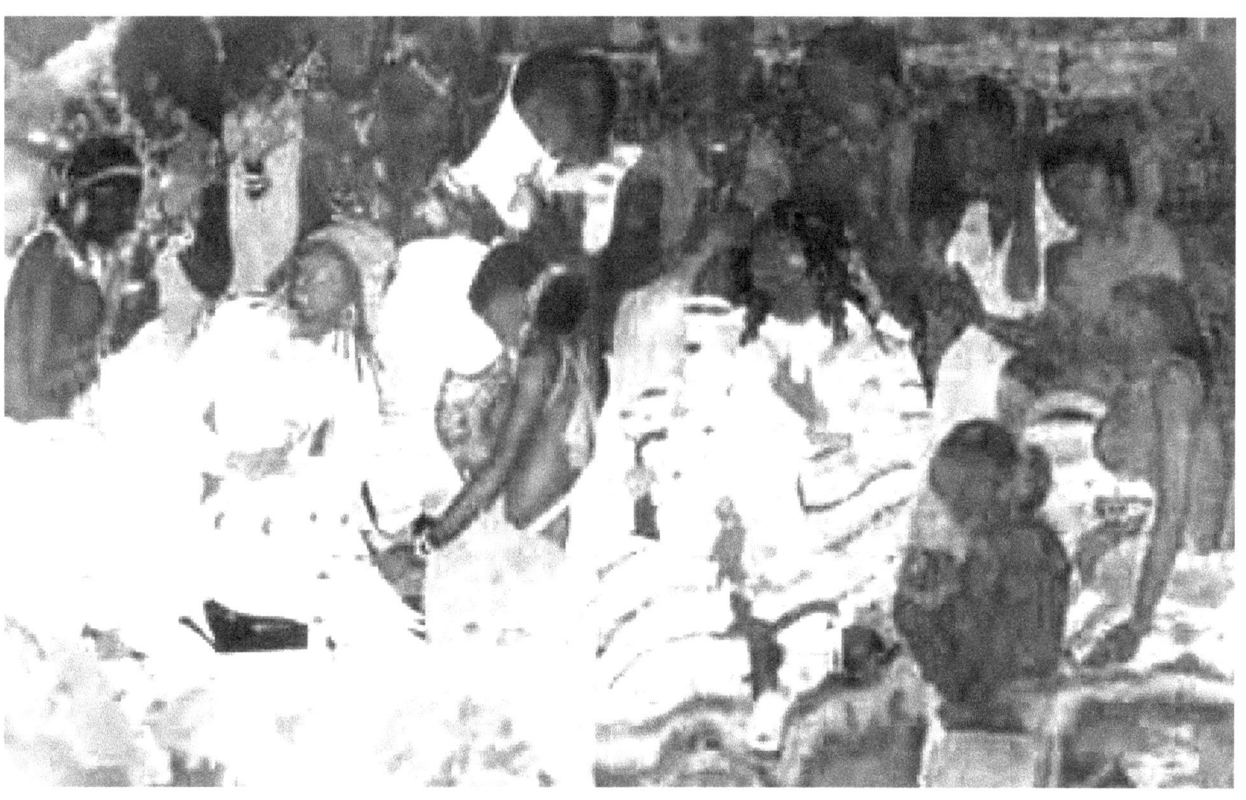

Figure 7 Bagh Cave 4 Dance and Music Arranged to Hold Mahajanaka Back

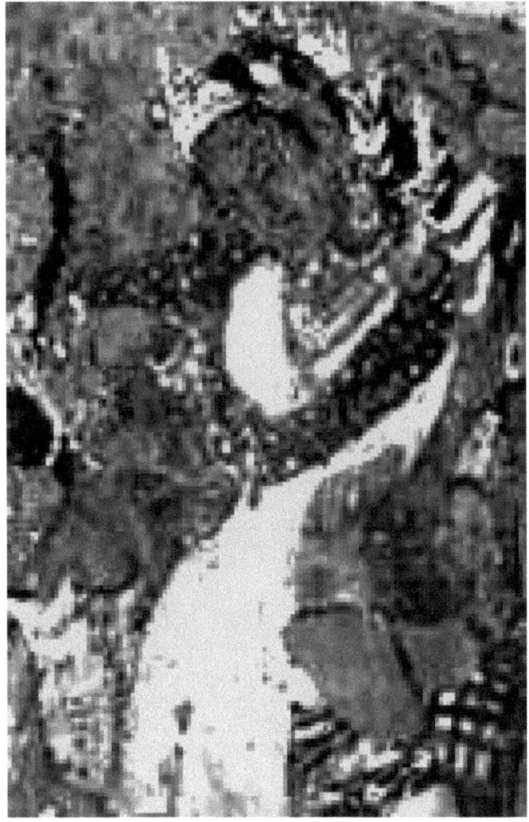

Figure 8

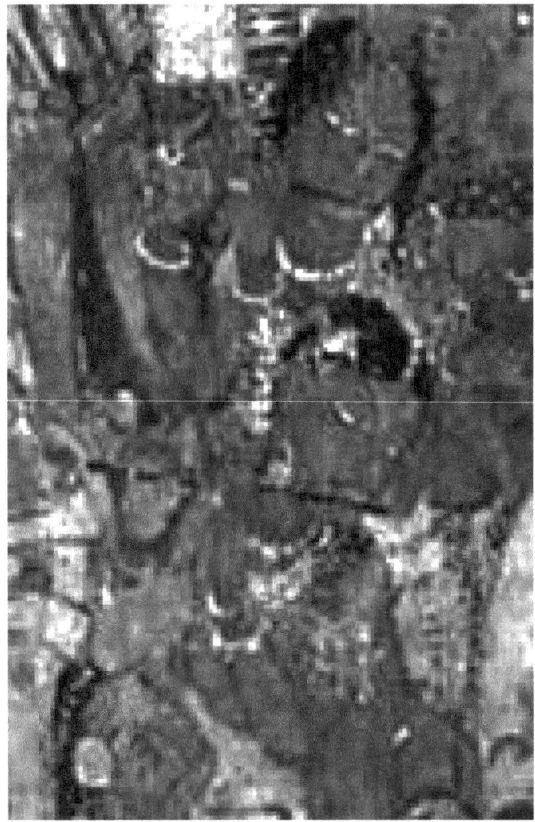

Figure 8a

Figures 8 and 8a Ajanta Cave 1 Dance and Music Arranged to Hold Mahajanaka Back

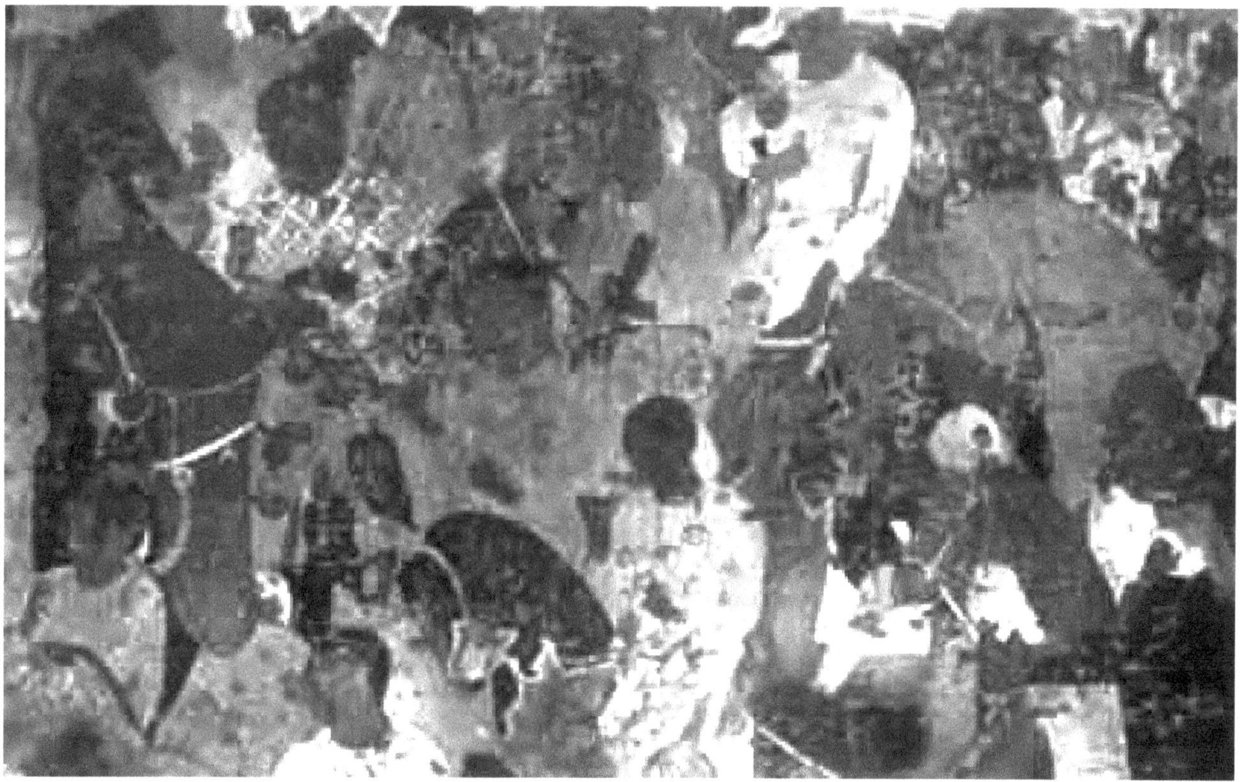

Figure 9 Bagh Cave 4 The Cavalcade

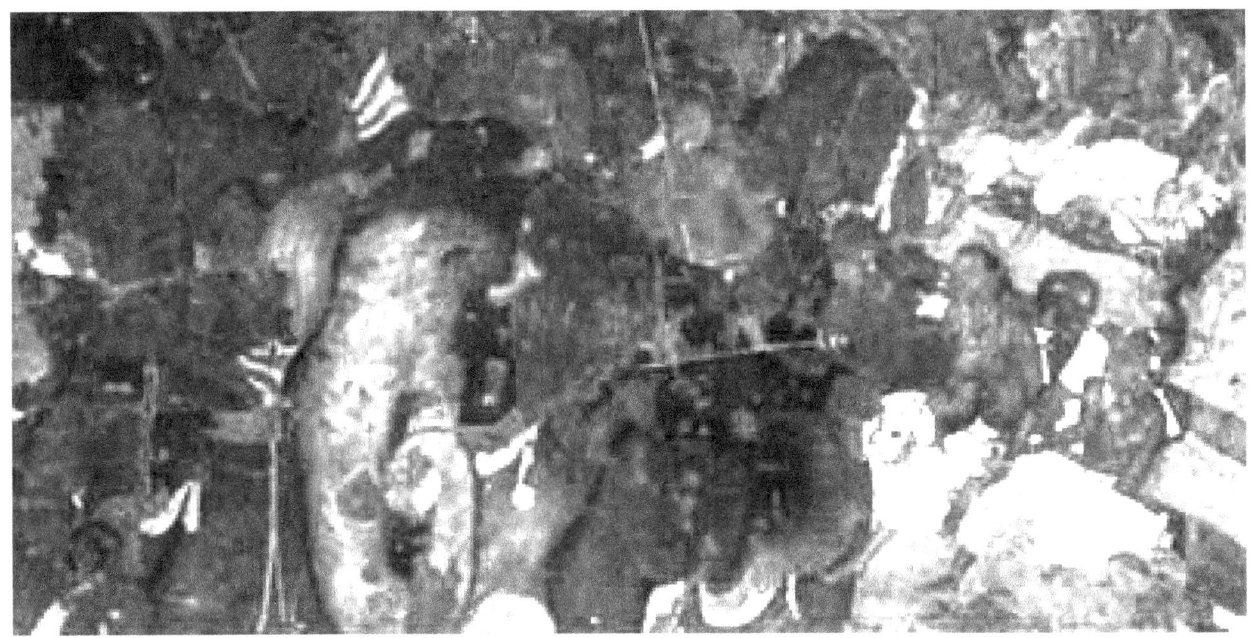

Figure 10 Bagh Cave 4 The Cavalcade

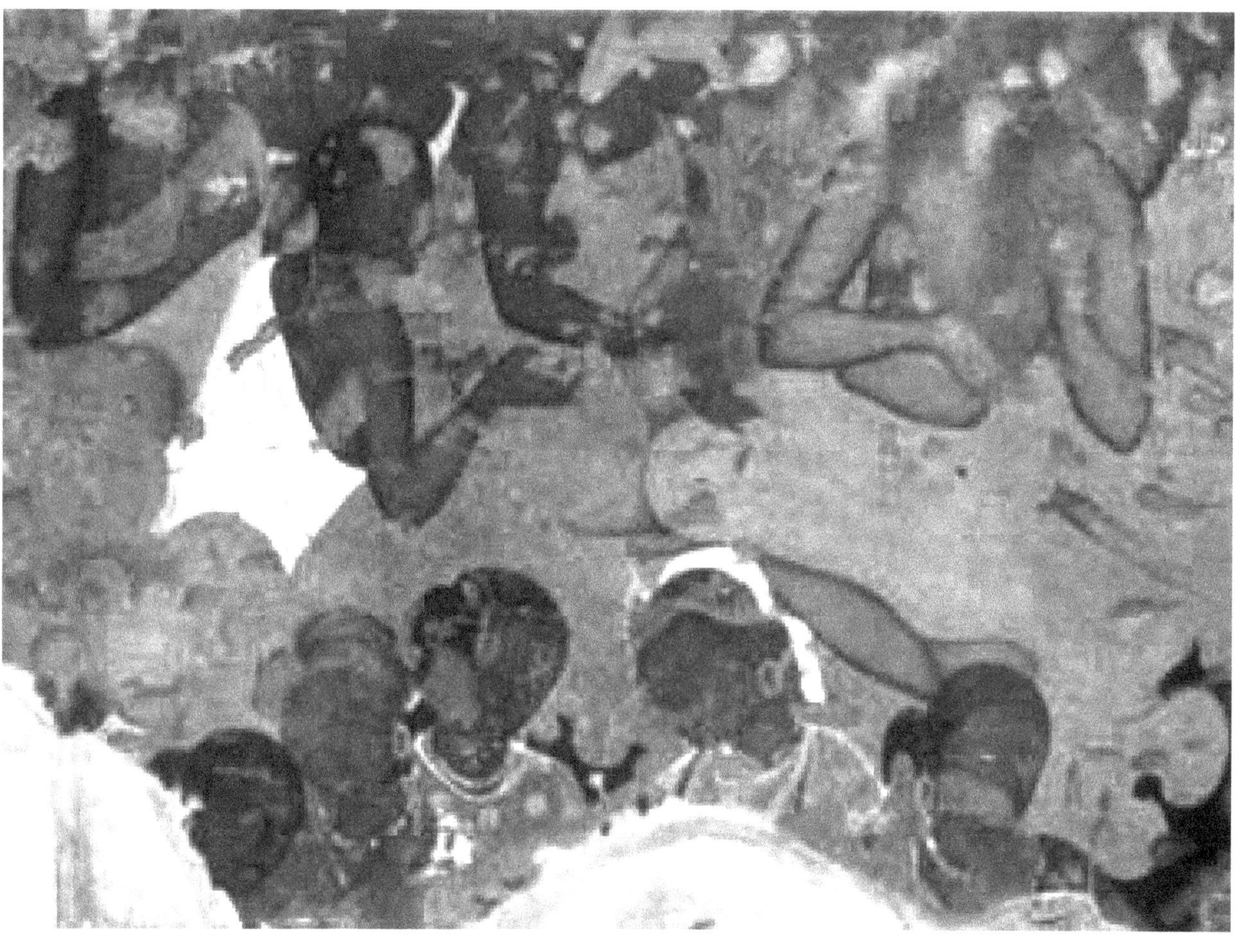

Figure 11 Bagh cave 4 Five Ascetics Flying through the Air

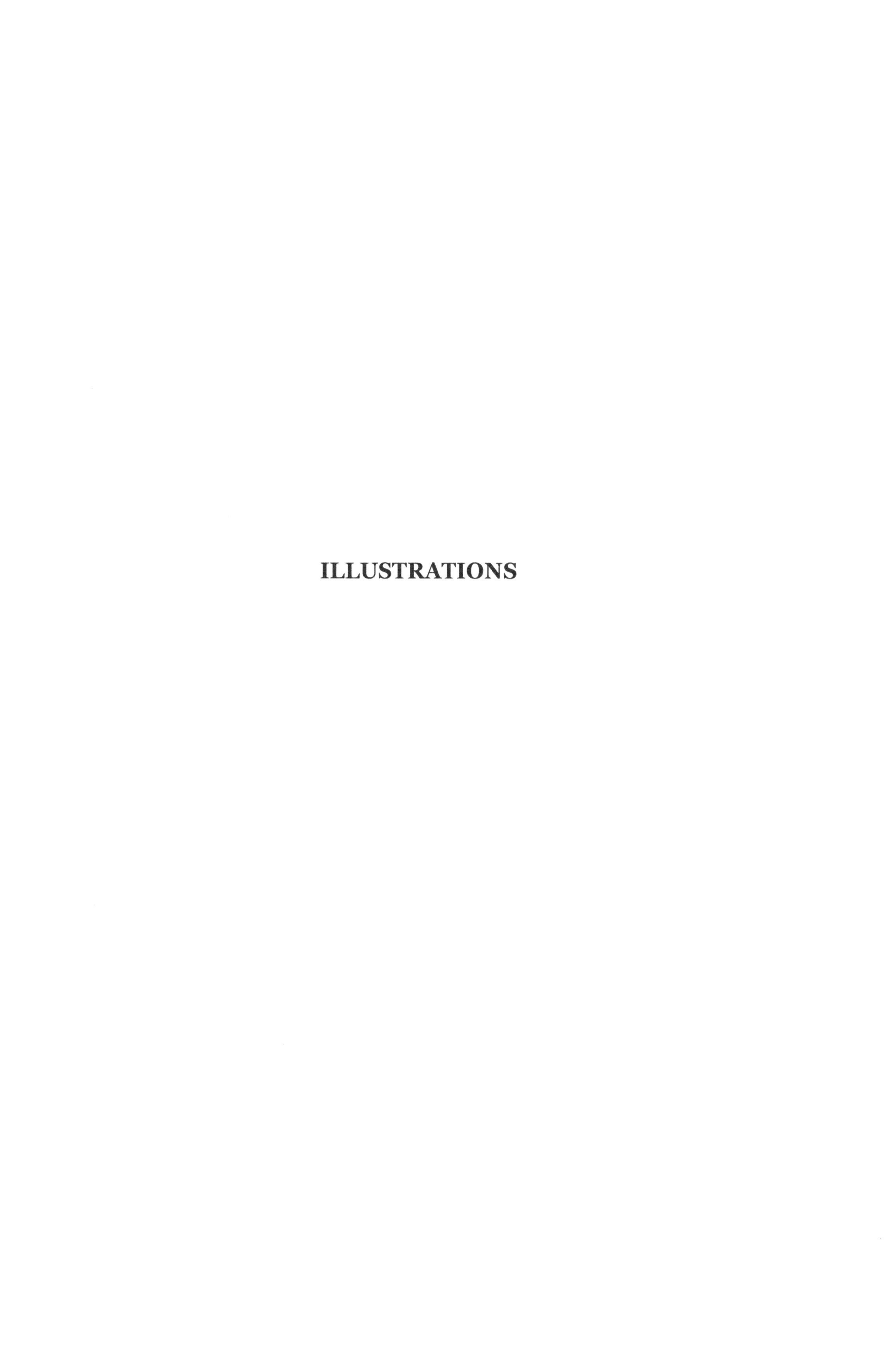

ILLUSTRATIONS

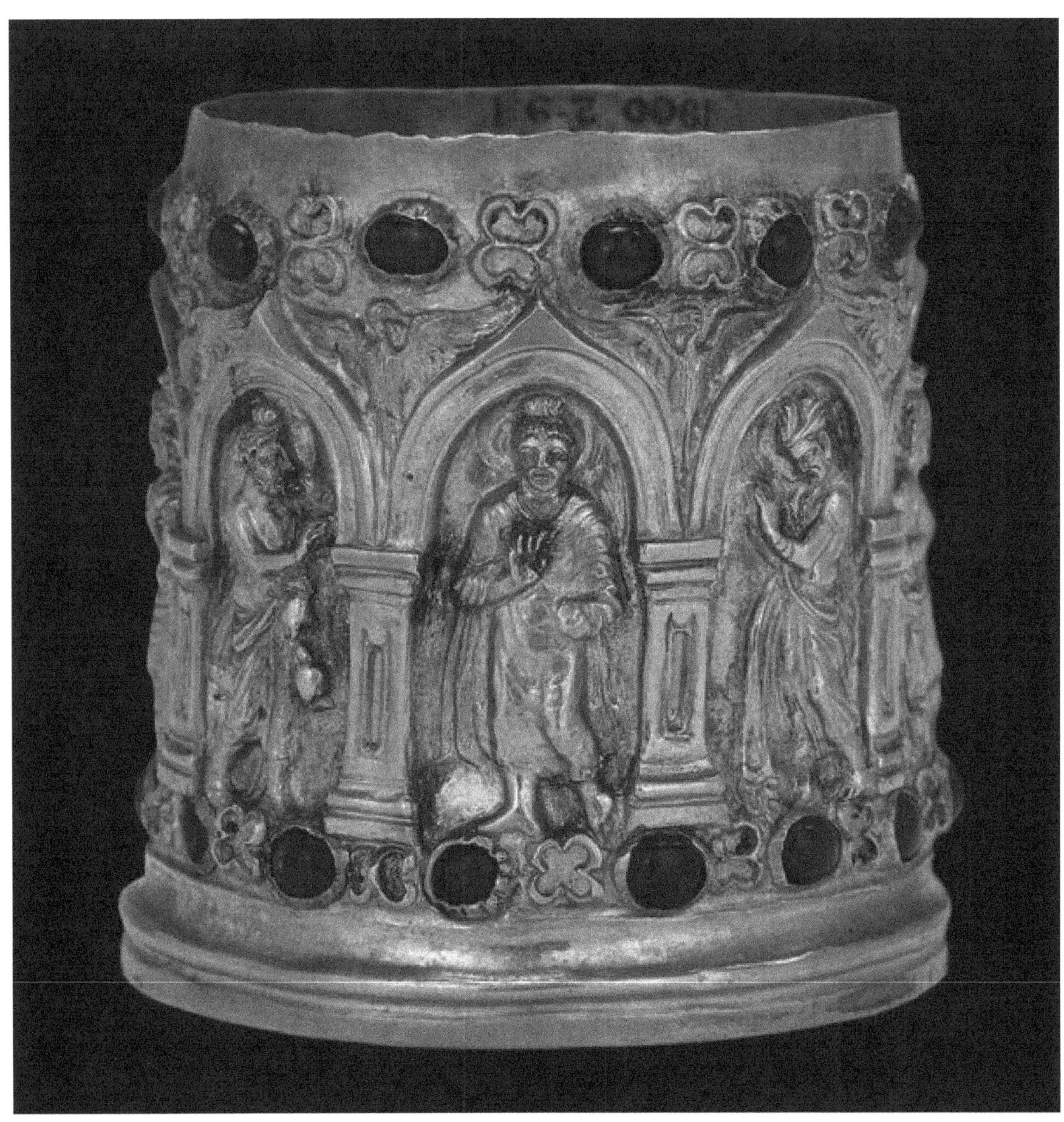

Figure A The Bimaran Reliquary, The British Museum

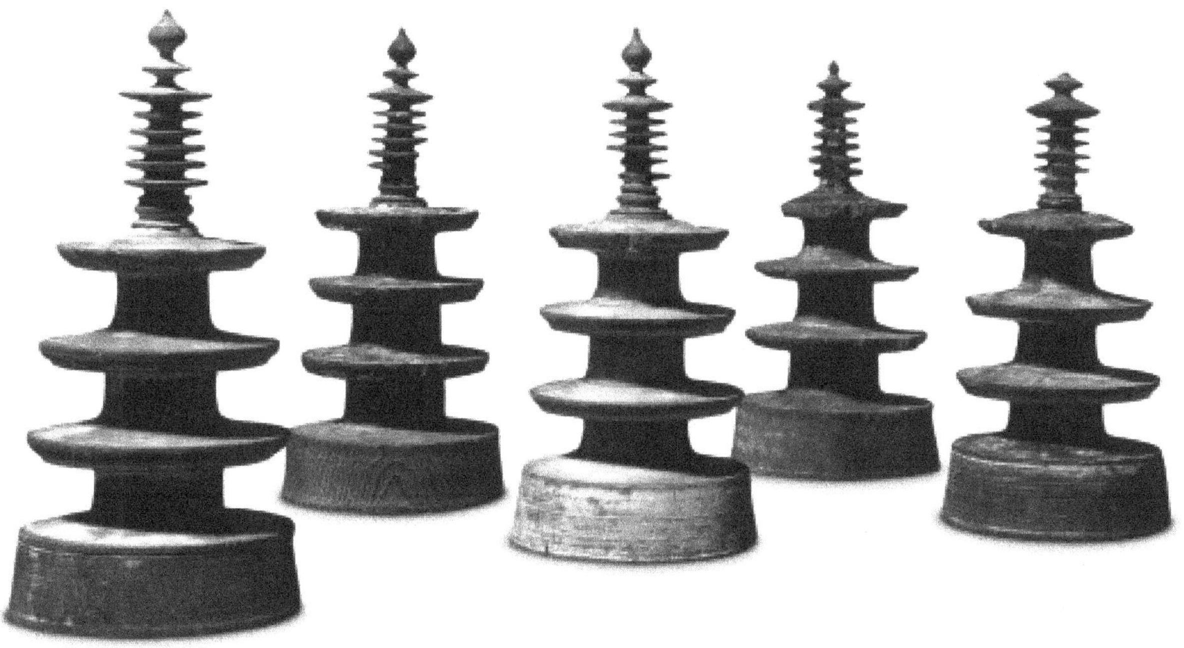

Figure B Votive Stūpas 8th century C. E. Japan The British Museum

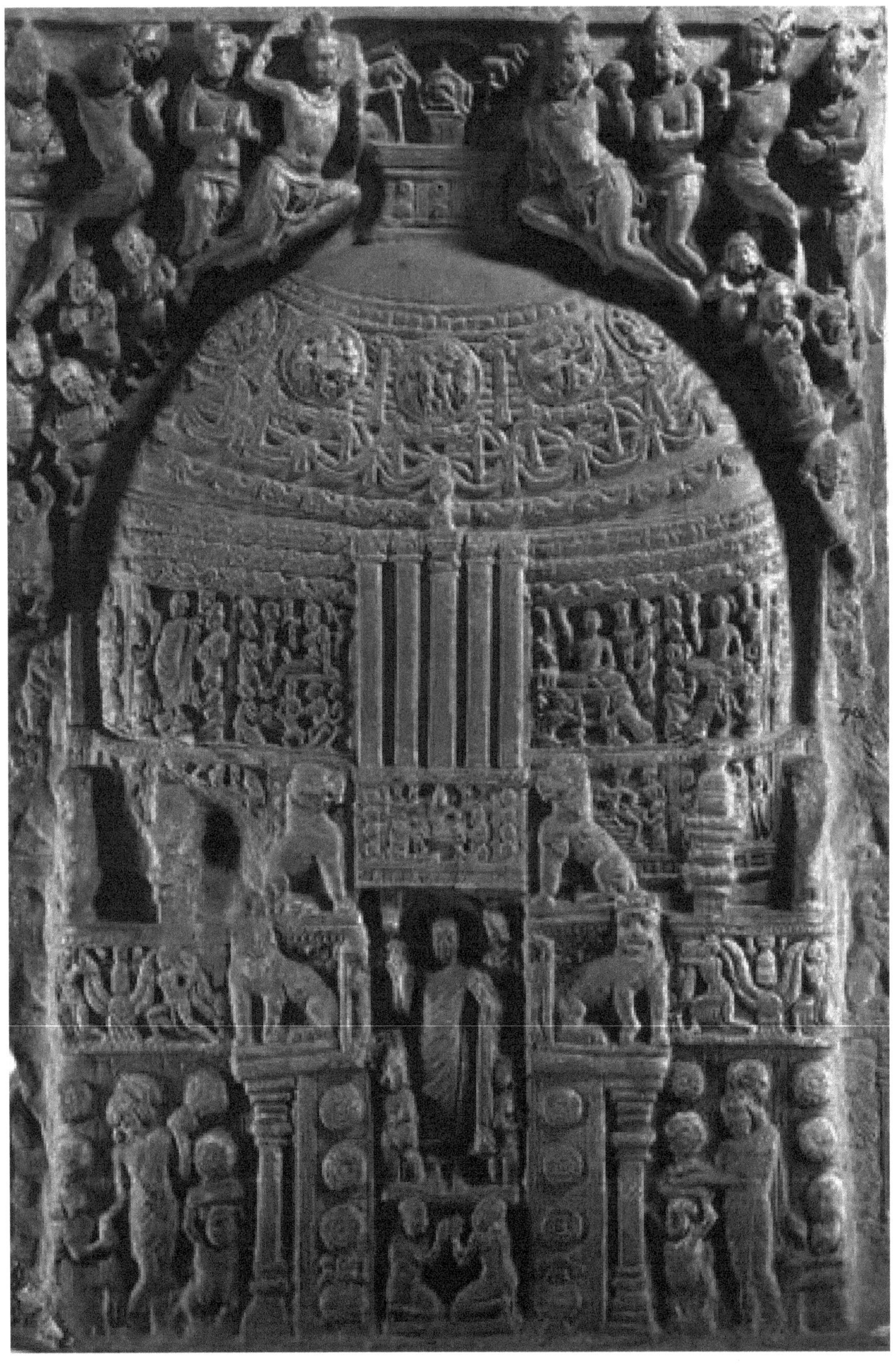

Figure C Adoration of Buddha on a *stūpa* Sculpted Panel Amaravati The British Museum: Courtesy Prof. Michael Greenhalagh

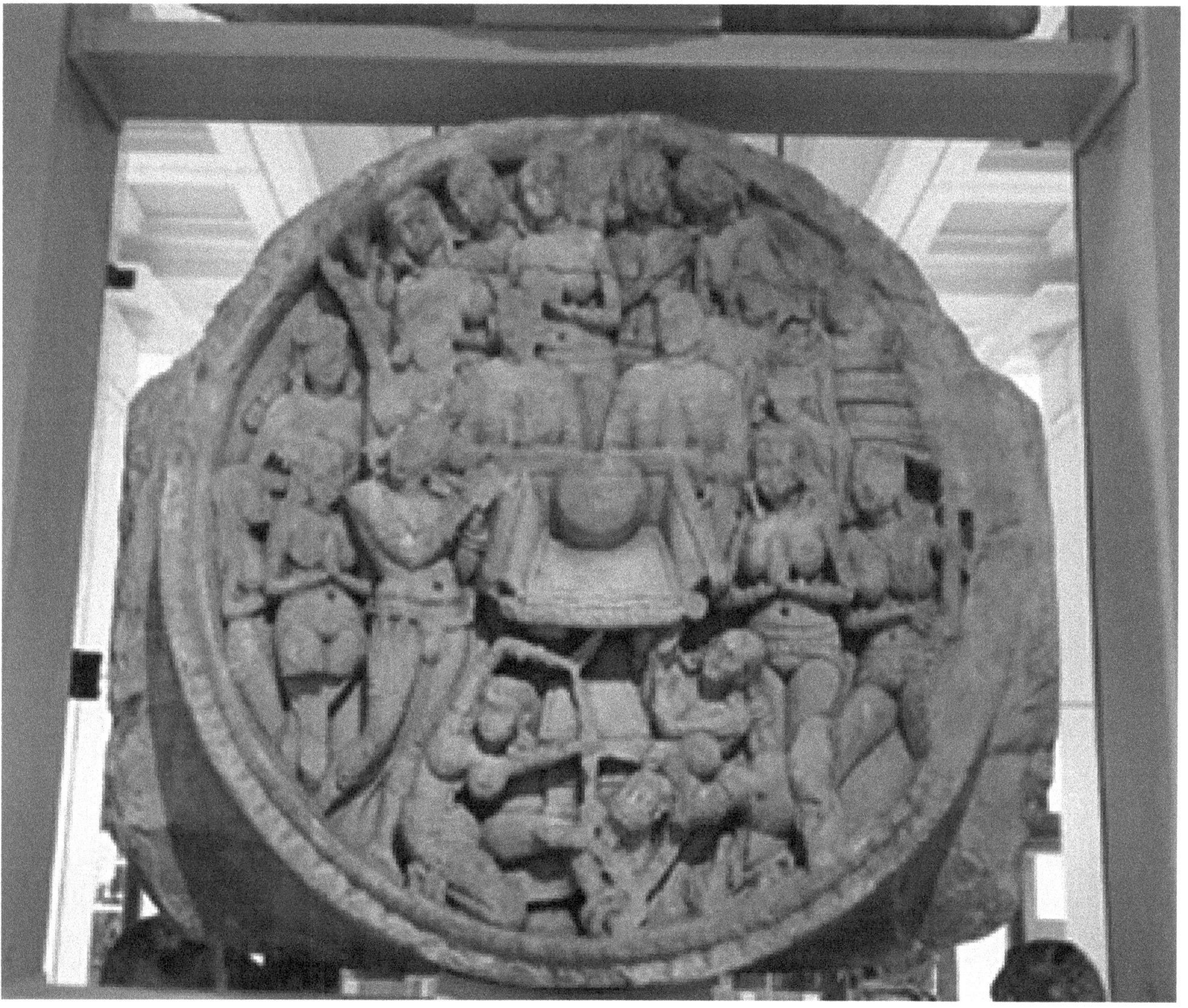

Figure D Adoration of Throne Symbolic of Buddha Amaravati
The British Museum: Courtesy Prof. Michael Greenhalagh

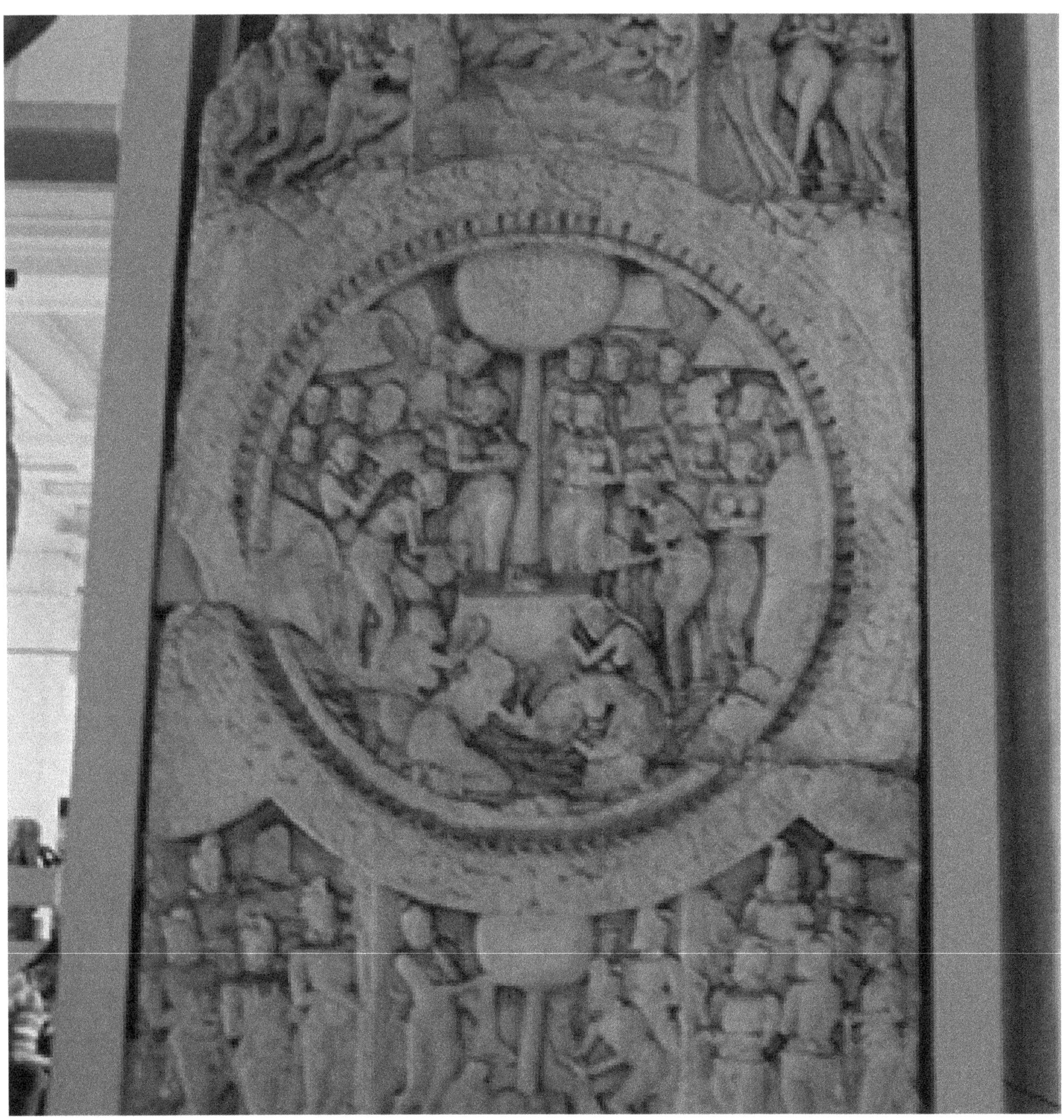

Figure E Adoration of Tree Amaravati The British Museum: Courtesy Prof. Michael Greenhalagh

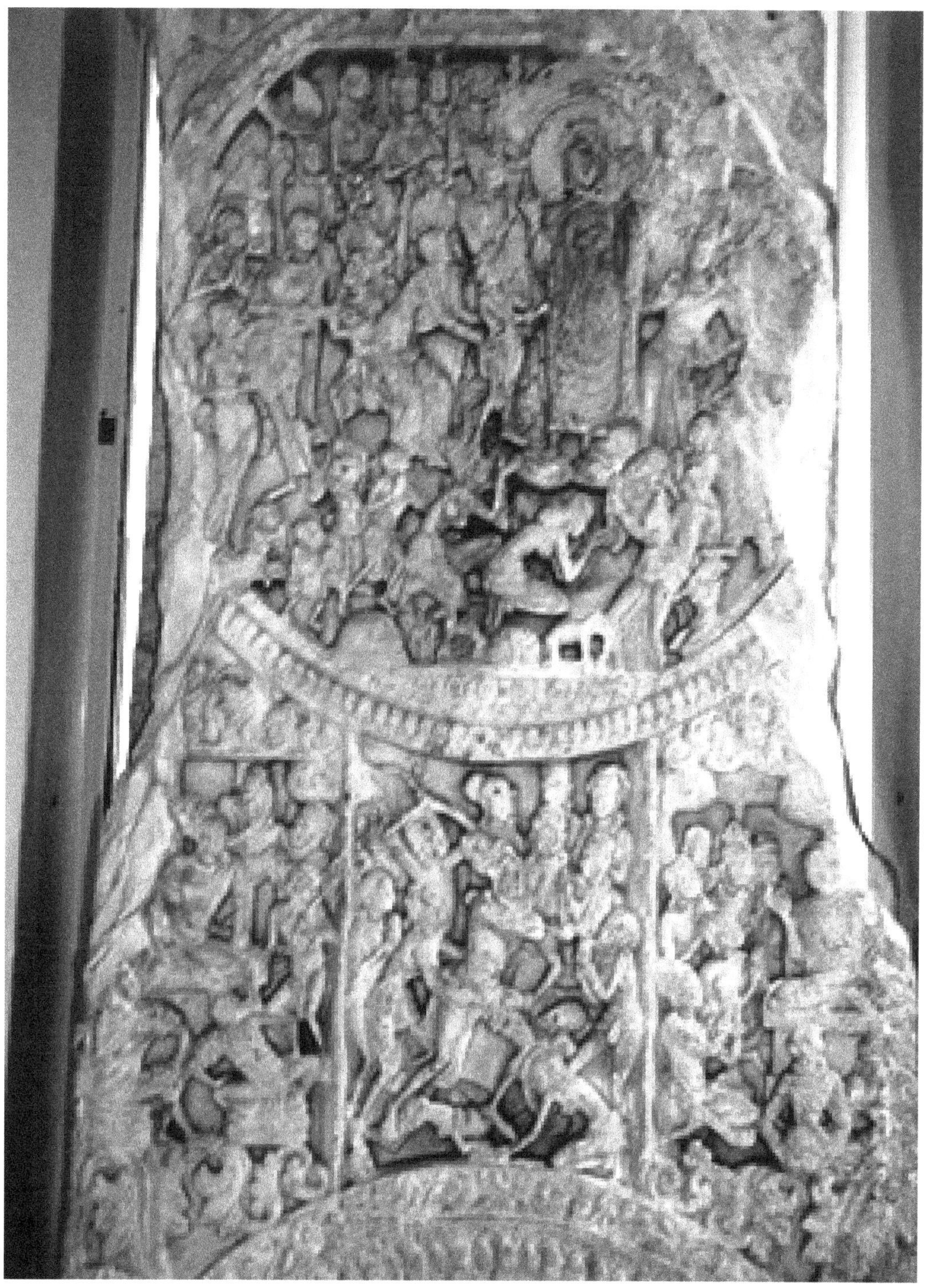

Figure F Adoration of Buddha Amaravati
The British Museum: Courtesy Prof. Michael Greenhalagh

BIBLIOGRAPHY

Primary Sources and References

Apte, V. S., *Sanskrit – English Dictionary*, Motilal Banarasidass, Delhi, 1988.

Census of India Reports on Dhar and West Nimar Districts, M.P. Series XI, 1981.

Chandra, Moti, *Chaturbhanis*, Bombay, 1959.

Corpus Inscriptionism Indicarum, Vol. IV, Pt.I.

Cowell, E. B. (Ed.), The *Jataka* Vol. VI, Motilal Banarasidas, Delhi, 1990.

Epigraphia Indica, all volumes.

Indian Archaeology – A Review, 1956-57, 1957-58, 1964-65, 1979-80, 1980-81, 1984-85, 1985-86.

Libert, Gosta, *Iconographic Dictionary of the Indian Religions,* Leiden, 1976.

Map Survey of India, Sheet No. 46.

Ramesh, K. V. & S. P. Tewari (Eds.), *A Copper-Plate Hoard of the Gupta Period from Bagh* Archaeological Survey of India, New Delhi, 1991.

Sircar, D. C., *Indian Epigraphical Glosary*, Motilal Banarasidas, Delhi, 1966.

Sivaramamurti, C., Citrasūtra *of the Visnudharmottram,* Kanak Publication, New Delhi, 1978.

Upasak, C. S., *Dictionary of Early Buddhist Monastic Terms (Based on Pali Literature),* Bharati Prakashn, Varanasi, 1975.

Secondary Writings

Anand, Mulk Raj, "Rhythm of Dance and Music in the Bagh caves", *Marg*, Vol. XXV, No. 3, June 1972.

Anderson, John, "Bagh Caves – Historical and Descriptive Analysis", *Marg*, Vol. XXV, No. 3, June 1972.

Barrett, Douglas and Basil Grey, *Treasures of Asia, Indian Painting,* Mac Millan, London, 1978.

Barthes, Roland, *Responsibility of Forms – Critical Essays on Music, Art and Representations*, Oxford and Basil Blackwell, London, 1986.

Barua, D. K., *Vihāras in Ancient India – A Survey of Buddhist Monasteries*, Indian Publications, Calcutta 1969.

Bhattacharya, A. K., Techniques *of Indian Painting,* Sarawat Library, Calcutta, 1976.

Bhattacharya, B., Indian *Buddhist Inconography,* Cosmo Publication, New Delhi, 1924.

Bhattacharya, P. K., Historical *Geography of Madhya Pradesh,* Motilal Banarasidass, Delhi, 1976.

Chaitanya, Krishna, *A History of Indian Painting – Mural Tradation,* Abhinav Prakash, New Delhi, 1976.

Chandra, Moti, Early *Indian Painting, Asia* Publishing House, London, 1970.

Chandra, Moti, *Trade and Trade Routes,* Abhinav Publications, New Delhi, 1977.

Chaudhary, Mamta, *Tribes of Ancient India,* Indian Museum, Calcutta, 1977.

Coomaraswamy, A. K., *The Origin of the Buddha Image,* Department of Ancient History and Culture, Univ. of Calcutta, 1970.

Coomaraswamy, A. K., *Elements of Buddhist Iconography,* Munshiram Manoharlal, New Delhi, 1972.

Das, S. T., *Life Style- Indian Tribes, Vol.* III, Gian Publishing House, New Delhi, 1989.

Dehejia, Vidya, *Discourses in Early Buddhist Art – Visual Narratives of India,* Munshirm Manoharlal, New Delhi, 1997.

Dey, Mukul, My *Pilgrimages to Ajanta and Bagh* Oxford University Press, London, 1925.

Dutt, Sukumar, *Buddhist Monks and Monasteries of India,* George Allen & Unwin Ltd., London, 1962.

Fyfe, Gordon & John Law (Ed.), *Picturing Power - Visual Depiction and Social Relations,* Routledge, London, 1988.

Getty, Alice, *Gods of Northern Buddhism, Clarendon* Press, Oxford, 1928.

Ghosh, A. (Ed.), *Ajanta Murals,* Archaelogical Survey of India, New Delhi, 1967.

Gupta, P. L., The *Imperial Guptas,* Vol. I, Vishwavidyalaya Prakashan, Varanasi, 1974.

Haldar, A. K., "The Painting of Bagh Caves", *Rupam,* VIII, 1921.

Harle, H. C., *Gupta Sculpture,* Oxford, Clarendon, 1974.

Impey, E. Esq. "Description of the Caves of Bagh in Rath", in *The Journal of the Bombay Branch of the Royal Asiatic Society,* Vol. V, Bombay, July 1856, reprinted, Germany, 1969.

Jain, K. C. *Malwa through the Ages,* Motilal Banarasidass, Delhi, 1972.

Kail, C. Owen, *Buddhist Cave Temples of India,* Taraporevala, Bombay, 1975.

Khandalawala, Karl, "Bagh and Ajanta", *Marg,* Bombay 1991.

Khare, M. D. *Bagh ki Guphayaen* (In Hindi), M. P. Hindi Granth Akademy, Bhopal, 1971.

Kramrisch, Stella, *Art of India,* Phaidon Press, London, 1955.
Lahiri, Nayanjot, *The Archaeology of Indian Trade Routes,* OUP, Oxford, 1992.

Law, B. C., *Geographical Aspects of Kalidasa's Works,* Indian Research Institute, Calcuatta, 1954.

Law, B. C., *Geographical Essays Relating to Ancient Geography of India,* Bharatiya Publishing House, Delhi, 1976.

Law, B. C., Geography *of Early Buddhism,* Bharatiya Publishing House, Varanasi, 1973.

Luard, Maj. C. E., "Gazeteer Gleanings in Central India – Buddhist Caves of Central India", Indian *Antiquary,* Vol. XXXIX, 1910.

Marshall, John, et al, *The Bagh Caves,* India Society, London, 1927.

Mode, Heinz, *The Woman in Indian Art,* Allied Publishers Pvt. Ltd., New Delhi, 1972.

Murty, K. K., *Glimpses of Art, Architecture and Buddhist Literature in Ancient India,* Abhnav Publications, New Delhi, 1987.

Pahadia, S. M., *Buddhism in Malwa,* Delhi, 1976.

Parimoo, Ratan et al (Ed.), *The Art of Ajanta, New Perspectives,* Vol. II, Books and Books, New Delhi, 1991.

Parimoo, Ratan, "The Myth of Gupta Classicism and the Concept of Regional Genres", in *New Quest,* Nov - Dec., 1990.

Payak, M. M., "Mushroom Paintings in Bagh Caves", Rupa *Lekha,* Jan, 1984.

Ray, Nihar Ranjan, *Idea and Image in Indian Art,* Munishiram Manoharlal Publishers Pvt. Ltd., Delhi 1972.

Ruseell and Hiralal, *The Tribes and Castes of the Central Provinces of India,* Vol. II, Anthropological Publications, Oosterhont NB, The Netherlands, 1969.

Saraswati, S. K., *A Survey of Indian Sculpture,* Munshiram Manoharlal, Delhi, 1975.

Sharma, R. A., *Technology and Material Life of Central India, Agam* Kala Prakashan, Delhi, 1991.

Sivaramamurti, C., *Sanskrit Literature and Art – Mirrors of Indian Culture,* Memories of ASI, Delhi, 1970.

Spink, Walter M., "Before the Fall – Pride and Piety at Ajanta" in Barbara Stoller Miller (Ed.) *The Powers of Art: Patronage in Indian Culture,* Oxford University Press, Oxford, 1992.

Tambiah, S. J., *The Buddhist Saint of the Forest and The Cult of Amulets, Cambridge* University Press, Cambridge, 1984.

Thapar, Romila, "Cultural transactions in Early India – Tradition and Patronage", *Radical Humanist,* Part I & II, February-March 1987.

Thapar, Romila, "The Social Role of Craftsmen and Artists in Early India", in Michael Meister (Ed.), *Making Things in South Asia,* Philadelphia, 1988.

Weiner, Sheila L., *Ajanta- Its Place in Buddhist Art,* University of California Press, Los Angels, 1977.

Williams, J. G, Art *of Gupta India,* Princeton University Press, New Jersey, 1982.

Winstedt, Richard, (Ed.), *Indian Art,* Oxford Book Co., New Delhi, 1947

www.ingramcontent.com/pod-product-compliance
Lightning Source LLC
LaVergne TN
LVHW070533110826
845147LV00017BA/981